SKIN DEEP

Women Writing on Color, Culture, and Identity

Edited by Elena Featherston

The Crossing Press, Freedom, CA 95019

Dedication

This book, as everything in my life, is dedicated to the courage, wisdom, and compassion of my mother, Willye B. Logan, who has never failed to nurture the truth of my Spirit even when she challenged the wisdom of my Ways. It is also dedicated to my daughter Alicia for all her struggles to BE whole which give me ceaseless lessons in change and the power of Spirit; my granddaughter Alexandria for teaching me compassion and reminding me daily how magnificent "wildness," life, and color are.

Photo Credits
Tracy Clarke by Stefan Maria Rother
Ehulani Kane by Jan Watson
Genny Lim by Bob Hsiang
Victoria Lena Manyarrows by Teresa Scherzer
Vanessa May by Tam Thompson
Daphne Muse by Donald Johnson
Saundra Sharp by Lawrence Hawkins
Sabrena Taylor by Dr. Alma Lowery-Palmer
Carletta Wilson by Eduardo Calderón

Printed in the U.S.A.

Library of Congress Cataloging-in Publication Data

Skin deep : women writing on color, culture, and identity / edited by Elena Featherston

      p.   cm.
    Includes bibliographical references.
    ISBN 0-89594-708-0 (pbk.)
    1. Minority Women--United States. 2. United States--Race relations. I. Featherson, Elena.
E184.A1S616   1994
305.4'0973--dc20
                               94-12506
                                CIP

Aknowledgments

I am deeply indebted to the following friends, relatives, and colleagues for their advice and support in midwiving *Skin Deep* into existence: Virginia R. Harris, often my partner in conspiracies of change; Kathleen Rountree for including her interview with me in her Crossing Press anthology, *Coming Into Our Fullness;* Elaine and John, my publishers, who took a chance on me and trusted me to do the job; Cara Page for her enthusiasm; Alice Walker for BEing (even her silences guide my steps along the path); Sister Maureen Hilliard who forced me to rethink the role of women in westernized religion; Stephanie Johnson for being there and lovingly calling it as she saw it; Jean Ishibashi for her fighting spirit and gentle heart; bell hooks for her scholarship and always telling like it was, is, and ought to be; Donna Jones for saving my sanity in Berlin; Andreas Klabunde for working so hard to understand his own racism, Mama for somehow sparing me the madness of colorism. Thanks to Darling Mata Villena for introducing me to the cross-cultural training grid; Starhawk for her generosity.

I would also like to acknowledge the energy and commitment of the contributors to this anthology, each of whom has enriched my life. Permission to reprint or excerpt from the following previously published and copyrighted works is gratefully acknowledged: "See No Indian, Hear No Indian" from *Two Worlds Walking,* New Rivers Press, 1994 by Victoria Lena Manyarrows; by permission of the author. "Yet You Worship Me" from *Typing in the Dark,* Harlem River Press, 1991 by Saundra Sharp; by permission of the author. "Growing Up Integrated—Did Momma Do the Right Thing?" first printed in *The Crisis Magazine,* Crisis Publications, Baltimore, 1988 by Saundra Sharp; by permission of the author. "Wanted" from *Cross Roads,* May 1993, by Demetria Martínez; by permission of the author. "Diaspora Salvadoreño" and "Salvadoran Diaspora" from *Cross Roads,* May 1993, by Martivón Galindo; by permission of the author. Translation by *Cross Roads.* "The Black Latin and the Mexican Indian" from *Cross Roads,* May 1993, by Avotcja; by permission of the author. "When I Awoke The World Was Dreaming" from *The Raven Chronicles,* Winter 1991–1992, by Carletta Wilson; by permission of the author. "The Custom of the Times" from *L. A. Weekly,* Vol. 13, No. 48, October 18–24, 1991, by Rita Williams; by permission of the author. "Truth Telling" edited from *Woman of Power* Issue 22, Summer 1992 by Joy James; by permission of the author. "Attending to Process" edited from *Woman of Power* Issue 22, Summer 1992 by Nora Hall; by permission of the author. "Believing in Ourselves" edited from *Woman of Power* Issue 22, Summer 1992

Contents

Part II
On Becoming *Ad*Normal:
Finding, Creating, and Accepting Wellness

Musing on Race and Color in America

"…Colorism—in my definition, prejudicial or preferential treatment of same-race people based solely on their color…colorism, like colonialism, sexism, and racism, impedes us."

"If the Present Looks Like the Past, What Does the Future Look Like?" Alice Walker from
In Search of Our Mother's Gardens

"In the U.S. different women of color have similar, but very different experiences of racism. We use the term cross-racial hostility to differentiate what goes on between and among women of color from racism. Racism is prejudice plus power—control of others' lives, power over. Cross-racial hostility is prejudice plus trying to feel powerful. Very different!"

"Developing Unity Among Women of Color,"
V. R. Harris and T. Ordona from
Making Faces, Making Soul

The catalyst for this anthology was a near disastrous altercation with a longtime colleague, collaborator, and friend. My friend and I are both dark-skin (now there is a relative term) African American women, and I am the darker, but our personal experiences with darkness, while similar, were also very different. We—politically astute women trained to help others appreciate diversity—almost ended a twelve-year friendship over an issue of color.

My friend grew up in a southern household where colorism was an ugly fact of life. Though essentially the same hue as her elder sister and younger brother, she was designated "the darkest." Her light-skin mother, dark-skin father and siblings used color like a stick to whip family members into a frenzy of discontent. Her uncles married light-skin women; her male cousins married white women. When she was growing up, being called "black" by another Black person was worse than being called a nigger. Told repeatedly that she was the "blackest" member of her family, my friend deeply internalized the idea that she was unattractive and less valued because of her hue.

My upbringing was different, the parental color dynamic was the same—light mother, dark father, but colorism was not part of our family life. My family, like hers, runs the color gauntlet (no, I do NOT mean gamut) from light, bright, and damn-near white to berry black. And as my half-sister says: "We are a pretty people; we just don't have ugly people in our family." My brother and I, always treated as valued, attractive people, escaped most childhood agitation about color. Occasionally, of course, we were called "black" by peers, but our response was, "Yeah! And proud of it!" We were not colorstruck. Befuddled, they left us alone.

"Colorstruck" is a term the Black community has used for generations, perhaps centuries, to describe people afflicted with the disease (disease) of colorism. But, unlike me, my friend had been struck by color, beaten with it so severely that the truth of her beauty was obscured. The reality of being in her skin became an agony she bore for most of her life.

I could not validate my friend's experience of darkness, and she could not credence mine. Negation of this type usually breeds cold contempt, and we were unexceptional. Hurt, confusion, isolation, and a misguided sense of betrayal—all the ingredients for a volatile confrontation—were present, but accepting responsibility for our own feelings and actions allowed us to see other options. Having grappled with so many differences—age, sexuality, personal style—during the course of our friendship, our shared struggle with the pain of internalized colorism was another opportunity to honor our individual truths.

BEing in our skin is a struggle for spiritual survival which people of color understand but often do not honor by acknowledging. In western-influenced cultures, skin is the great significator. It is the first thing people see and is used to define who one is and to what one can "rightfully" aspire. The privileges, or lack thereof, attached to different shades of skin, texture of hair, shape of eye or gender are encoded into the social fabric. More than we care to admit, our socialization often makes us complicit in living out myths devised by others. Our Authentic Selves are lost; we behave as though our realities are only skin deep.

We are members of a society that mythologizes the legacy of western "civilization" in our lives and rewards those who distance themselves from their ancestral roots, original language, native foods, family names, spiritual traditions, and personal truths. The resultant alienation is then used to strengthen the argument that people of color have more in common with the whites who colonized, captured, conquered, or commodified them than with one another or the ways of their forbearers.

On Bill Moyer's television series *World of Ideas*, Toni Morrison said:

"Black is the glue that holds America together." She went on to make the following statement:

> *"To make an American, you had to have all these people from all these different classes, different countries, different languages feel close to one another. So what does an Italian peasant have to say to a German burgher, and what does an Irish peasant have to say to a Latvian? You know, really, they tended to balkanize. But what they could all do is not be Black. So, it is not coincidental that the second thing every immigrant learns when he gets off the boat is the word, "nigger." In that way, he's establishing oneness, solidarity, and union with the country. That is the marker. That's the one. Well, these were people who were frightened. I mean, I would be. You go to a strange country, maybe you have some friends there. You need a job. You've cut your bridges. You've said something is terrible back home. You go, and you emigrate, you go someplace else. And if it's under duress, you are facing chaos. And when you are facing chaos, you have to name it, or violate it, or control it in some way. So you want to belong to this large idea, you want to belong. And one learns very quickly what to belong to. And you belong to this non-Black population which is everywhere. But it serves. It serves. It has always served economically a lot of forces in this country."*

Color is the ultimate test of "American-ness," and black is the most un-American color of all. This is not to suggest that other racial and ethnic groups in the United States have not, do not, and will not continue to suffer the vagaries of racism and its extant oppressions. Yet these same groups are permitted to share in the American legacy of being not-Black/ black. This is a powerful, privilege and a slippery psychological prison. It encourages Black people to believe that their oppression is *the* one by which all other oppression must be assessed. The pattern also prompts every oppressed group in America to gauge its success in the battle for equity by measuring it against that of Blacks. "You cannot say/do this to Blacks, but you can say/do this to me? It is not fair!" The treatment afforded Black people in American society defines the state of its democracy. It also suggests that the status of Black people is the measure of the lowest standard for the treatment of human beings; the country accepts the premise that no one should be treated as badly as Black people.

There is then an unspoken commitment between oppressed and oppressor to define human rights in terms of "race" and color. In such conditions, despite blood-sacrifice, hard-work rhetoric, scholarship, and rebellion, how much equity can anyone hope to attain? What is the price of resistance?

Yet the concept of separate "races" on a continent where African, Asian, European, and Indigenous peoples have been "race-mixing" for five hundred years is a precarious one at best. Many Americans cling to the myth of racial purity that racialized myths, lies, half-truths, and distortions are among America's most perverted assortment of secrets.

James Baldwin said in *The Price of the Ticket*, "…it is exceedingly difficult for most of us to discard the assumptions of the society in which we were born, in which we live, to which we owe our identities…" This idea is critical to understanding why, as the people most affected by oppressive behavior, we engage in colorism and cross-racial hostility, "acting out" the worse aspects of the racist system from which we struggle to extricate our humanity.

Fundamental change, as opposed to temporary legislative remedy, has not taken place in America because the same economics, history, labor, law, literature, philosophy, politics, and religion that established prevailing doctrines justifying racist barbarisms is taught to people of color and whites alike. As Dr. Frances Cress Welsing says in her "Color Confrontation Theory," being taught the "patterns of emotional response, perspective, and symbols" of one's oppressor brings one's mind under the control of said oppressor. These patterns are never accidental; they embody a culture's deepest assumptions, structures and power relationships. Hence, people of color have been carefully trained to serve the needs of whites and to disregard their own, becoming in the process second-line guardians of white supremacy.

Change *demands* that we discard the assumptions of this society; it means actively questioning our culture and our identities. It can be terrifying to take apart one's personality in this way, but mercifully, people of color are expert interpreters of multilevel realities—our survival depends on it.

The following concerns reoccur in conversations with women of color about BEing in our skins and alliance-building: (a) the common, but varied oppressions experienced by people of color; (b) the psychological damage caused by ongoing conspiracies of denial concerning the true histories of people of color and white people; (c) the need to understand race and ethnicity as defined by our experience and to chronicle them in our own voices; and (d) the desire to construct *ad*normal (ad—a motion toward, a nearness to, truly normal) behavior and create wellness; (e) the construction of alliances and institutions built on foundations of mutual respect.

Skin Deep is intended as a primer for those whom playwright and educator Glenda Dickerson calls "contrary women": women of color who want to understand the struggles of other women of color; women of color who want to form alliances/coalitions with women of different national, cultural, racial, or ethnic origins; women of color looking for ways to heal from the unhealthy behaviors of white western culture; women of color who want to explore the intersections of oppression as it is experienced by different groups; and for anyone who wishes to alter the oppressive, ethnocentric, and patriarchal behaviors so deeply woven into the fabric of America.

Activist, educator, and organizer, Papusa Molina makes a telling distinction between coalition and alliance. Coalitions, she says, are temporary, often single-issue covenants, formed with specific goals in mind, and as such need to be disbanded as soon as the objective is achieved. Alliances, on the other hand, are a manifestation of our shared visions of a better society for all people.

Every work offered here—even those bordering on analytical—is intensely personal and grounded in individual experience. They resist "mainstream" attempts to depoliticize and trivialize the value of true multicultural debate. Race, gender, sexuality, and language are of necessity areas of struggle for women of color. Crossing the borders of literary form, moving in and out of languages and linguistic style, the contributors of *Skin Deep* scrutinize the institutions, traditions, and conventions, that attempt to silence their voices, render their perspectives irrelevant, and shackle them.

For women of color re/membering ourselves is a daily act of courage, a ritual of survival. We live "theater of the absurd," understand at least two languages, speak in a variety of voices and view the world always from at least two perspectives. We are forced by circumstance—and driven by passion—to construct, dismember, and reconstruct our many Selves in the search for our Authentic Self. We are compelled—in order to heal the damage to our souls—to amputate the cancerous growth of negative assumptions imposed from without and to create internal referents which define our Truths from within.

Re/membering is a form of resistance; it is a life-affirming and self-defining act. Re/membering is a cry of defiance in the face of that which would steal our past, predetermine our future, cut short our present, challenge our humanity, render our lives meaningless, and make us invisible. It is our refusal to be silent, our rejection of oppression.

This book is divided into two sections. The first, "The Paradox of Color: Living in an *Un*sane World," considers the emotional amputations as well as the spiritual powers derived from the struggle to BE in our skins.

The second, "On Becoming *Ad*normal: Finding, Creating, and Accepting Wellness," suggests ways of unlearning destructive behaviors and attitudes that affect people of color, and moving toward self-defined emotional, mental, physical, and spiritual health.

There is no homogeneity—cultural, ethnical, ideological, or racial—among women of color in the United States. We have strong historical similarities: we are not white, we are not male, often we are not Christian. We are Other. But the state of our Otherness is unique by group, and as individuals. We need to "scratch our purple spots," acknowledging our mutually inflicted pain and our cross-racial hostility, in order to forge viable alliances. Thus, as you read the works offered here, meditate on your own stereotypes about other people of color and your internalized oppressions; "listen with intent to hear" the voices of your sisters. Risk being made to feel uncomfortable—confusion and ambiguity are facts of life for us all. You may find healing and comfort in another woman's words. Hopefully, you will find insights that can be taken into your daily life as part of the struggle for equity.

Contrary to popular mythology, issues of race and color are *not* as simple as Black and white—or Red, Yellow, or Brown and white. The most important dynamic is the relationship of people of color to one another. We have passed through one another's lives too often to ignore this. Seeking to frame questions of race and color as fully as possible, women from the mainland to the islands, academic and nonacademic, indigenous, immigrant, and "native-born," were invited to address their individual truths. The women represented here are African, Asian, Sephardic Jew, Latina, Middle Eastern, Native Hawaiian, First Nation, and admixtures thereof. Styles vary. The work of women who have never written before complements the works of published writers and theorists. "Traditional" uses of capitalization and other literary conventions have been redefined and subverted by writers to enhance their voice and to emphasize cultural difference in language use.

I choose not to smooth over our differences in order to create what literary critic and educator Barbara Christian describes as "a nonfunctional homogenous group identity." Structuring an anthology that encourages us to be more accessible to one another was my goal. But no matter how many ideas and perspectives have been included in this volume, others, due to space constraints, have been omitted; we are far too heterogenous for that not to be the case.

While this book will hopefully appeal to a broad audience, I have no interest in "taking the edge off" the feelings expressed by women of color to make them more palatable to others. To do so would be to dishonor our diversity and minimize our realities. Readers are invited to share in our dialogue with one another, not to direct it. For as Barbara Christian once said, "If we write only with the 'other' in mind, then we will not be writing about ourselves, but of that 'other's' view of us. That means that we will not be able to develop."

Your ideas are valued; please address your comments and suggestions to:

Elena Featherston
c/o The Crossing Press
PO Box 1048
Freedom, CA 95019

Yours in Sisterhood,

Elena Featherston
San Francisco, California

March, 1994

Part I

The Paradox of Color: Living in an *Un*sane World

The conditions of life in America have had a devastating impact on the lives and minds of people of color. Fraud, theft, economic reprisal, emotional and psychological abuse, and open physical violence remain daily facts of life. The motives for the violence vary, but most of it occurs in the interest of maintaining white supremacy and white-skin privilege. This is the harsh, unvarnished, inescapable truth. What have we done about it? What shall we do about it?

In this section, women express their thoughts and feelings on questions of race- and gender-related history, realities, joys, and discontents. Their works explore the extraordinary price of living between realities as members of a culture that insists there is only one reality. In these works women weep, break silence, demand respect, promise revenge, sip the waters of rage, ponder the circumstances of their birth, class, sexuality, and color. They are sometimes totally outrageous, often reflective, surprisingly gentle, and in the most unexpected moments, filled with humor. But these are all steps along the road to understanding our collective circumstances.

Norma Soto, 1956

Woman of Color

Norma Elena Soto

the ad called for women of color
and I had to ask myself,
does Chinese, Mexican,
Spanish and French
make me a woman of color?
I asked a co-worker
because I was not sure.
She said, definitely yes!
I dye my hair purple
to cover the grey
and to stir up interest.
It looks black except
there is a purple haze
around my head when
the sun is behind me.
My body is stocky,
and my green eyes slant
when I laugh or smile.
Those are the only outward
signs that might convince someone
that I am a woman of color.
My co-worker
had to explain to me
that the Chinese and Mexican
does it for me.
But, should someone
see my white skin and
question my credentials,
how would I prove
my qualifications?
I could smile
to slant my eyes,
speak Spanish and disclose
my Hispanic name…

maybe pick up an accent
and start bowing a lot.
Yet, somehow, those
whose business it is
to identify women of color
might doubt me.
My sister and I
have the same parents,
but she looks Arabic
with black hair, olive skin,
and flashing black eyes.
Same genes, different packaging.
Would she find herself
in this dilemma?
And what is so special about
this woman of color?
Me.
American born with
Mexican heritage in
a bilingual household.
Tiny strains of Chinese
culture filtered down
through two generations
to add a little spice.
That must be it.
Yes, I am a woman of color
standing proud and tall
at five foot three
ready to be counted
having myself right

And in the end,
would anyone care enough
to ask?

Norm Elena Soto lives in San Mateo with her two teenage children and is employed by the State of California.

Identity is a simple word yet it raises many complex issues and causes introspection. We grapple not only with ourselves, men and other women, but also with broader influences of history, society, cultural heritage, and traditional structures.

—from Making Waves

Virginia R. Harris, age five

Prison of Color

Virginia R. Harris

"In the passionate rhetoric about white supremacy what I hear missing is the fact that we believe in, have internalized, our own inferiority."
—Virginia R. Harris statement

"Colorism—prejudicial or preferential treatment of same-race people based solely on their color." I would add: Colorism is to ascribe value and privilege to a same-race person based on lightness of color.

Clarence Thomas's stated preference for light-skinned women is colorism. A 1989 lawsuit brought against a dark-skinned supervisor because of alleged color discrimination by a light-skinned woman was colorism.

When my eighty-year-old aunt, who dyes her hair, tells me I am too dark to wear my hair its natural gray, that is colorism (as well as ageism). Underdeveloping the pictures of dark-skinned people in my college yearbook so no one looked too dark was colorism.

The phenomenon of ascribing worth based on color is generally attributed to African Americans, but colorism is active among all groups. In every group there are variations on color, with "value" rated on lightness of hue. Blond and blue-eyed Aryan is "preferable" to "swarthy" southern European. Traveling in China, I observed that the light Chinese were the Party members and functionaries, the dark Chinese were laborers and farmers. The Chinese assigned our group of eight American women rooms based on color (two dark-skinned African American women in one room, one light-skinned African American woman and a Chinese American in another, two blond white women in a room, two brown-haired white women together, and two white women with almost-black hair in the last room). In New Mexico, the Hispanics I met were adamant about not being Mexican and touted their Spanish (read white) heritage. A Filipino American friend, whose parents are Filipino, who was born in the Philippines, was told by darker Filipinos that she was "too light to be Filipino." Light skin is prized. The belief that dark is evil, inherently less intelligent, and immoral is internalized. People of color don't seem to recognize this as another racist divide-and-conquer tactic. By engaging in colorist behavior we collude in keeping white supremacy in place.

I have done considerable work to be aware of and rid myself of internalized racism. I am conscious of the many overt/covert/subtle ways internalized racism determined how I navigated a world bent on my destruction. I was, therefore, surprised at the extent and depth of the pain and hurt triggered by writing this paper. As much as racism from whites or cross-racial hostility from other people of color hurts, my deepest hurt came at the hands of those who are like me—colored—Negro—Black—African American.

One night during the summer of 1991, watching television, I heard the following: "Black is the glue that holds this country together." My immediate reaction was, YES! A further thought: Hatred of blackness will tear this country (the world?) apart. We live in and by a racial hierarchy with black at the bottom. No matter how bad things get, all non-blacks can unify around that fact, can hold still another truth to be self-evident—*they* ain't black. Richard Pryor, in the seventies, did a monologue on how the Vietnamese emigrants were taught English. The first word learned? Nigger. The audience howled. I laughed too. The truth of his statement still stares us all in the face.

My father used to say, "You can't throw mud on someone without getting your hands dirty." So, if I am glue, you are either glue or stuck to me. The *best* glue is invisible, flexible, does not deteriorate, has no odor, is nontoxic, and dries clear and fast. That definition aptly describes the image I tried to portray for many years, while at the same time fighting with every ounce of strength not to be held in my "place"—invisible, cohesive, and unshaken by racism (or any other form of oppression, for that matter). Racism and its legacy colorism made me struggle to be something I am not—white and male. I straightened my hair and tried to lighten my skin, while denying what I was doing: "I use Nadinola (a bleaching cream popular in the fifties and still advertised in Ebony) because it's the only thing that controls these blackheads." No pun intended. It didn't work. I was still female. I was still dark.

When I was growing up, calling someone black was worse than calling them nigger. We sat on the porch steps, and in a terrible game of degradation, compared our colors. Who was the darkest? Who was "it"? I was, more times than not. I fought my sister and brother because they called me black. I generally got beaten up in those fights, and then beaten again by my light-skinned mother for my loud, violent, attention-getting behavior. No matter the provocation, I had acted BLACK. The insidious irony is I am not darker than my brother and sister; I was made to THINK I was. Not only was racism outside waiting to rip me apart, the legacy of racism was active in our house. How did this come about? Why was it so important to make distinctions that don't exist?

My eyes itch from unshed tears. My parents' venom, born in their issues with color spewed out—hidden, unspoken, violent—inside our house. I learned not to cry when I was hurt or in pain. My mother was the beat-you-until-you-cry type. I "showed" her. I could take the worst she could dish out—without crying. A victory, I thought.

A little history: My mother's father, one son of a slave and her master, blamed his mother for the circumstance of his birth. (None of his children could tell me her name.) He hated white people and dark-skinned people. He could have "passed" but never did, to my knowledge. Even though he married a dark-skinned woman, he told his children not to marry dark because black was evil and no good. All his sons complied. One daughter complied; another daughter married a dark-skinned man, divorced him, and was mistress to a white-skinned black man for over forty years. My mother didn't comply, but when angry with my dark-skinned father, she said, "I should've listened to my father."

From the time I can remember, everyone was described by color, down to a half or quarter shade *darker* than someone else. If the person was dark, the description was negative, *especially* if the person was female. If for some reason the woman deserved a compliment, it was followed by "…but, she's so dark." "Marry light and improve the race" was the unequivocal message. All the men on both sides of the family in my parents generation married light-skinned women. My father's "other women" were even lighter than my mother. All my male first cousins married *white* women. What a difference a generation made! To this day all my mother's sisters say color was not an issue in their family.

I got the message: no good, dark, ugly, not worth black men's attention, unattractive, and not wife material. I believed it. "I'll show them" became my watch phrase. I might be dark…but you wait and see. I excelled in school. The man I married, to whom I was "superior" by virtue of class and more education, was lighter than me, had all the necessary credentials (degreed professional), and paid me minimal attention. When my sister met him, she asked, "How did *you* ever get a man like that?" She, on the other hand, married two very dark-skinned men. "The blacker the berry…" she used to say. But was she trying to be the lighter one and, therefore, "superior" to those men based on her color? I wonder.

Black has been the glue that kept me stuck in a prison, and in being victim. I am a dark-skinned woman who internalized the negativity society teaches about darkness. My internalized racism, colorism, and sexism have shaped an existence that I can only call a prison of color. I wanted to be impenetrable, not feel the pain. So, I built walls to protect myself. They have gotten thick over the years, and I am tightly bound inside a hated cell—my skin color. A posture created to "protect" myself from the excruciating pain of being black in a world where "biases…subscribe…Blackness as non-good 'Otherness.'" The walls were my armor against the world where I did battle against everything, with everybody. The walls held me in place; I restricted me like a girdle. Self-hatred is the tightest girdle anyone wears. I've been walled off, boxed in by my color, restricted in ways that are becoming clearer.

My prison—both protector and enslaver. Each wall familiar, like a face I remember but can't recall the name. I pace this enclosure until I recall the names. ANGER. That's easy—smooth as glass, cold to the touch. I turn a corner. INVISIBILITY. A contradiction learned early—a wall of distorted mirrors. Another corner, INADEQUACY. A well-paved, smooth wall requiring constant maintenance to keep the image of inadequacy at bay. Another corner, another contradiction. OVER/UNDERACHIEVING, a wall of different sizes and kinds of broken rocks set in the cement of control. The plight of a smart little black girl, simultaneously applauded and slapped. ANGER and INADEQUACY confront each other as do INVISIBILITY and OVER/UNDERACHIEVING.

I search for solace in this place that "protected" me in the past. But it feels so different! I thought the jagged edges, the hot acid rage were covered, hidden forever by the layers of control plastered over them. The internalized value system that states I am less than human because I am a descendent of Africa oozes out like pus from an infected cut. I've lived with the pain of being a woman, being black, being a victim, being hated, being angry, being invisible. I have survived in a world bent on my destruction. But if I am to be free, I must know these walls and for what they stand.

ANGER—a friend—the only emotion allowed in my family. Righteous anger covering a pool of helpless, hopeless rage so close to the surface but rarely expressed. All the hurt and pain I've suppressed about how I was/am perceived and treated because of my color came screaming to the surface as I engaged with another dark-skinned woman to write this paper about colorism. I felt such rage (at her) I was unable to breathe. Rage burst to the surface because a dark-skinned woman had had a different experience with colorism than I had. I was catapulted back to my childhood where fistfights and worse were common fare.

My reaction in the present recalled an incident: Seven African American women talked about how color had affected our lives. We varied from beige to black-brown (the color we used to call "African" when we were ignorant of Africans' color variety). All seven of us had experienced the pain of being the "darkest" at one time or another. Two had also experienced being the lightest. The black-brown woman was enraged. None of us could know or understand the kind of pain she had experienced. It was clear to me, at the time, that she needed to be *the* victim. I thought her rigid and closed-minded. All of us had painful experiences with colorism, but she was unable to allow any of us our pain because hers was so intense.

Six years later, I found myself acting out the same rigidity and closed-mindness. My friend's different experience with being dark-skinned did not "validate" my pain. My pain felt even more intense in comparison. The more we talked about our very different experiences with being dark-skinned black women, the more enraged I became. I held on to my old and new pain tenaciously, placing the blame for *all* that pain on my friend. Not only was my hurt very deep, my need to hold on to that hurt was as deep. I needed to be *the* victim, and I needed *my friend* to be responsible for my victimization. My parents and the community that hurt me when I was a child were gone. The system was too big and unyielding. If I allowed a different experience with colorism, somehow I would be erased—not just the invalidation of my experience, but an erasure of SELF. Erasure slams me into the wall of INVISIBILITY.

We African Americans are all colors. While racism distinguishes between us from dark to light, we still somehow become all the same. We are interchangeable in some instances, in others not. It depends on the use the dominant culture has for us in the particular moment. Hollywood cast Sidney Poitier as Thurgood Marshall in a made-for-TV movie, thus erasing the white-skin privilege Marshall had traveling throughout the South in the forties and fifties. *60 Minutes* aired an exposé about a New York employment agency's discrimination against blacks. The two African Americans who brought the suit were dark. The agency, to prove the charges were false, gave a light-skinned black woman the "privilege" of recanting the charge. The abject pain on her face as she tried to rationalize a corporate memo that clearly implied, "Discriminate, just don't get caught" was heartbreaking. How did she deal with that pain? Did she beat herself up, search for all the ways she failed? Did she make other black people responsible and render them invisible in order to feel she had some power? Was she able to hold it together so her bosses wouldn't know how she felt?

It is devastating when your illusionary world comes crashing down. The worst images reflected in those distorted mirrors haunt you. Feelings of INADEQUACY jump up like ghoulish Jacks-in-the-box, unexpected and terrifying. This wall's smooth surface is an illusion. INADEQUACY is wet tar that gets all over your best dress, and you weren't even conscious of being near the wall. As I struggled to erase the belief that I was inadequate, I simultaneously erased pieces of mySELF. If I couldn't be a white male, the only thing that would make me "adequate," I would best them at their own game—be more efficient, faster, take on more projects. I stood up to the power structure at work (all white men), ignored my pain and hurt. I felt most adequate (powerful) when I proved white men (and later white women) wrong, using their own data and the statistical methods I'd learned in their universities, only to get stuck once again in the tar of INADEQUACY when the racism and sexism were dismissed and I was ignored. What had I done wrong? How could I make them see? Civil Rights bills and executive orders provided some recourse for unfair treatment in the workplace. But what was the recourse in my life? I stood, feet sealed in cement, dodging feelings of inadequacy but getting pummeled over and over again.

I built an elaborate system of musts and shoulds, none of which left me room to breathe, to BE. I stood rigidly on the "American" principles I had been taught even if white people didn't. I became the champion for causes of race and gender while denying how I was used by those in power to keep people of color and women under control. My option? Prove that the together, competent, get-things-done image was the real me.

The jagged rocks in the wall of OVER/UNDERACHIEVING are splattered with the tar of INADEQUACY. We were taught in childhood that we had to prove we were twice as good to get ahead. Education was the key, so the more education one had… By the time I left graduate school, unable to find a job, I was saying, "Twice as good to get half as much." It was clear to me that getting a Ph.D. had more to do with endurance than with ability. When I finally got a job in my field, my abilities were measured by the kind of research I did—but the kind of research I was assigned came through a white man's race/gender filter. If I completed a project quickly, it was scrutinized for mistakes, accuracy double-checked.

After twelve years of "research" it dawned: Just because I majored in chemistry, I didn't have to work in it for the rest of my life. "How can you give up the prestige of chemistry for a job in personnel?" I was asked. I never felt the "prestige" chemistry was supposed to afford me. All I felt was rage at being a glorified dishwasher. They told me I couldn't switch from science to administration, so I showed them. In personnel I saw the records documenting a history of extensive racism and heard my boss argue to pay a person of color (or woman) less money. My boss asked me, "Who do you think you are? What makes you think you have the credibility to make these kinds of charges?"

Twenty years later racism is alive and well. "This is a country where racism has been the longest-standing national neurosis." Without racism, colorism would not exist. I obscured my pain about colorism by fighting hard against racism. I thought if I fought hard enough, the pain would go away. It didn't. Writing this paper brought all the feelings to the surface with an intensity I never experienced in the past. The armor I'd worn against the pain no longer worked. I had no scapegoat or object for the feelings. They were real. They were intense. They were mine.

I maintained two stances in the world. The outward one conquered obstacles, projected an "in charge" IMAGE. The inward one, a battered, dark-skinned child who believed she could do nothing to be acceptable, whose identity was her victimization. I wanted to be warm, protected, loved, and nurtured. I wanted a womb. I built a prison. I can continue to internalize the hatred I've learned from my family and the society. I can continue to turn it on myself and those like me. I can continue to envy those lighter than me, feel superior to those darker than me. I can continue to be an instrument of my destruction.

Yes, I could. But I choose to live a conscious life, making conscious choices to BE a whole person. Rejecting the value system—in which self-esteem and self-worth are based on being "better than," where as an African American woman I am defined as "less than"—would seem easy. But the power of the glue of hatred is greater than I ever imagined. It is a full-time, life-time job undoing my socialization. I am learning to embrace all facets of who I am, to embrace a SELF rooted in BEing equitable in my soul, learning to nourish well-being and differentness in SELF and others.

Virginia R. Harris is a fifty-six-year-old African American who works with individuals and groups in transition. She has been a chemist, a human resources manager, and is now an organizational dynamics consultant, facilitator, writer, and quilter.

Victoria Alegria Rosales, age eleven

The Other Half of Me

Victoria Alegria Rosales

I am the so-called "Furiosa," a nine-year-old.
Got two younger brothers.
When I was born I ate my mother's insides,
or so she said when I was five.
Every time I make her angry, she reminds me of it.
She tells me that's why my brother Rico, seven,
is fat and misbehaves and why Mico, five,
was born with a hole in his heart.
Her teeth got rotten, and she was no longer pretty.

Mama gives the boys hugs and kisses.
Buys them toys.
I don't care.
The dog licks my face.
The cat gives me hugs.
The baby chicks play with me and shit all over my dress.
The boys aren't allowed to go outside
because they may catch colds.
I can roller-skate around the block.
No neighborhood boy can catch up with me.

"*Maricona*," shouts a neighbor boy
who wanted to defeat me as the roller-skating champ.
I run furiously to the roof. I'm mad.
I want to crack the boy's *coco*
but if I do, my mother will be angry.
She tells me I'm the reason why she takes those little pills
that make her sleepy all day.
"You're just like your papa," she yells.
My papa is big and fat and drinks "cuba libres."

"Ugh!" I taste one.
Mama drinks them too.
Then they lock themselves in their room.
My mama laughs and cries a lot.

I don't know what to do.
When she comes out, she eyes me
as if I have done something wrong.
I rush to the roof, hungry for something,
but I don't know what for.

Mama stuffs bit of liver into Mico while Rico awaits his turn.
Mico spits up the meat.
She forces the liver down his throat.
He sobs.
"Don't you want to grow up to be a strong man?" she asks.

A cat chews up the afterbirth of her newborns.
Can't understand my mama.
"How could I have eaten up her insides?"
I wonder, tasting my oatmeal.

From the moment I was conceived my mother knew there was something terribly wrong with her pregnancy. But it took her two months before she decided that the best thing to do was to have an abortion. The lump in her stomach was not that of a normal child, she later told our family. This creature kicking and growing inside her was a descendant of Manuel, that half-breed whose manners were those of his people, the Indians who frequently descended from *el cerro* (the hill) into Guadalajara to sell their wares. It had taken her over six months to teach Manuel not to spit on the sidewalk. Hadn't anyone ever told him that he should spit on a handkerchief instead?

Although abortion was condemned by the Catholic church in Mexico in the early 1940s, as it still is today in the 1990s, there were doctors who would perform a first-class abortion for a fee of one thousand *pesos*. For seven hundred *pesos* my mother could have had a second-class abortion performed by a doctor who only found clients among the poor. And for three hundred *pesos* my mother could have found a medical student. My mother managed to borrow two hundred *pesos*, but even the midwife, learned in the arts of herbs and sorcery, refused to help. My mother, she said, was too far advanced in her pregnancy to abort me. The only consolation the midwife could give was to tell her she wasn't the first woman to give birth to an unwanted child. When my mother became hysterical, saying she didn't want to give birth to the child of a dark father, the midwife consoled her. "What if the child turns out to be a boy?"

My mother, Estrella, which means "star," blamed the gardener—a peon, hired by her rich relatives, who had ejaculated his seed, which grew into his creature, something different from those of her social class and status. The idea of a dark-skinned child frightened her. To have a dark-skinned baby was to be always poor, forced to live in the worst of neighborhoods. Who was going to rent to her if they thought the child's father was an Indian with skin the color of night? No one. Not even the Pope would rent to a white woman who had violated the codes of white people. There was a saying, the same in Mexican culture as in English-speaking culture: "You have made your bed, now sleep on it." What was she going to do?

Because my mother was a dispossessed, penniless widow who had lost her wealth and status, her rich relatives took her in. She soon realized that in order to live with them she must shine my uncles' boots, empty my aunts' chamber pots, and feed the *perros*. (This she didn't mind because she always liked dogs.) She didn't want her cousins as her *patronas* but agreed to live with them because she wanted Bonita, the child from her first marriage, to continue being a rich and spoiled little girl. But after two years of servitude my mother was ready to tell her rich cousins to stick all their millions of *pesos* you know where. She also had lost hope that a man from her class would marry her. She realized that the *señoritos* of her class overlooked her beauty to get engaged to less attractive, and sometimes much older, women from monied families.

Then my father appeared. He was the most recent peon hired to work for them. "Manuel may be the answer to my prayers," my mother thought.

My father offered to marry her when he found out she was pregnant. He blamed himself for putting me in her womb. He was determined to give me his name—the thought of my mother giving birth to an illegitimate child hurt his pride. So my mother took this opportunity to end her servitude. She wanted a home of her own where she and Bonita would never have to be servants again. Once she had moved to a poor neighborhood and was no longer eating steaks or drinking wine, she regretted her decision.

Although my mother considered leaving my father hundreds of times, she just couldn't do it. If my mother left, who was going to support her? True, Manuel could only provide her with frijoles and tortillas. (This is a lie. My aunts, from my father's side, brought my mother food. But my mother considered my aunts' contributions *desperdicios*, leftovers.) Who would pay the rent, buy her clothing? If only she had retained her upper-class privileges, she would have been able to buy herself a government appointment. She knew nothing about politics, as is true of many politicians in the world, but a fee paid in cash would have ensured her a position.

My father's sisters suggested that my mother pray and confess every day, take communion on Sundays, and bathe with blessed water until she gave birth. My mother, although she hated her sister-in-laws for being poor, uneducated, and almost fanatically religious, and although she really didn't believe in the teachings of the Catholic church, tried to follow this advice because she hoped to bear a son. Perhaps a son would be the solution to her problem.

One day my pregnant mother heard of Soledad, who lived not far away. Nine years before, Soledad had conceived Siamese twins. Intrigued, my mother set out to look for her. But when my mother finally visited her, she wished she hadn't. Soledad lived in the worst kind of poverty, poverty as monstrous as her twins who shared the same torso. Indeed one head was white and the other black. My other was poised to run away as quickly as she had come, to borrow the seven hundred *pesos* for a second-class abortion from her sister, Luisa, when the light-complexioned boy spoke in a high-class Spanish. "Señora," he said, "please don't be frightened." She was enchanted. The other head just stuck out his tongue at her. Was courtliness in his genes? my mother wondered. Later my mother would recount this meeting, swearing he impressed her not because of his light complexion, but because he was born so courtly, so gifted. (The dark-headed head never liked my mother. I don't blame him.)

I know there were other reasons my mother didn't go to her sister for the abortion money. For one, Luisa had told her not to expect any help if she married my father. For another, she was certain that she was going to bear a son. (And, after me she did. Two. Mico and Rico.)

Perhaps there was another reason my mother decided to forget about her abortion. She became so fascinated with her discovery of the two-headed boy that she forgot about her own situation. Finding Antonio Jr., as she later baptized the white-skinned twin, was like finding a lost relative. From that day on, she made a point to educate the white-headed boy—and did everything possible to stop Jesus, the dark-headed boy from picking on his brother. As Soledad was always very busy with her other children—Estrella's visits made her feel obligated to stop washing diapers to talk, as if my mother was the *patrona*—my mother would bring books to read to Antonio Jr.

Every night my mother asked herself, what had convinced her to marry Manuel? Had he bewitched her with his sexuality, so different from that of her first husband? Now she understood why low-income women bore so many children. She wouldn't become one of them, nor would she ever allow Manuel to raise a hand to her as Soledad's husband did to his wife.

Estrella ofttimes found Soledad bruised from beatings inflicted by her husband. When she consulted Antonio Jr., he said it was because his father was drunk: "He gets upset because he cannot earn enough money to feed all of us." It must have been at this moment that my mother decided a life of frigidity rather than pleasure. Later my father would accuse her of becoming cold and distant like the rich, spoiled white *patronicitas*.

Although Antonio Jr. and Jesus had a "dog-like" body, it didn't matter to my mother. They were still boys. She spent so many nights wondering how she was going to help Soledad get out of her poverty, she forgot about her own.

One day, she saw an advertisement for a circus coming to town. It occurred to her that if the boys were hired by Circus Vargas, the family's poverty might end. She still had relatives who would help her, who would see to the details of getting the boys hired if notified that she had found a freak. She would have liked being the boys' manager, but big-bellied with me, she could not.

When Estrella blurted the idea to Soledad, she was surprised to hear her answer. Soledad didn't want the world to see her children as abominations of God. "Never, señora, never," she swore. Later my mother would compare Soledad's position with the stubbornness of a mule. "Imagine," she would tell her friends, "she refused, preferring to live in the ghetto."

Before this fight ended their friendship, my mother had agreed to be the light-skin boy's godmother. A *comadre* had to be found to be the godmother of the dark boy. My mother taught the dark-headed child not to yell obscenities, not to bite and spit at his other brothers and sisters. She also scolded Soledad for letting them grow wild like animals, showing their *pipi*, "so typical of poor families."

The priest had to be bribed and given a *mordida* to baptize the boys. My mother used some of the *pesos* she had saved for the abortion to pay the baptism. And, of course, my mother chose the names. The light one was baptized Antonio, after her first husband, and the other was Christianized with the name Jesus. (My mother had to pay the priest another fifty *pesos* because he didn't want the dark-headed child to be baptized with the name of God.) The baptism took place when the church was closed.

Much later, after I had been born, my mother used to recount how difficult it was teaching Jesus good manners—and, of course, how Antonio Jr. never did anything wrong. Stamping her foot, she would tell her society friends (by this time she had divorced my father and returned to her sisters, taking me along as an unpaid servant) how hard she had worked to break the boys' habit of kissing. As I served the ladies coffee, tea, and their *panecitos*, my mother would go on and on telling how, when the twins were fatigued, the two heads entangled in long, passionate kisses. This disclosure was too much for some of the white-skinned ladies who drank coffee holding the cup with their pinkies up. Some gave little cries of horror and coughed into their white handkerchiefs. Then they giggled like little girls when hearing how the other siblings screamed and threw buckets of water on the two heads to separate them, "as people do to animals when they are stuck in the act of coitus."

But this hadn't stopped the kissing. Proudly my mother would tell how she had suggested to Soledad that each time they began to kiss she offer one of the boys something he liked. The trick worked. While Antonio sucked on a popsicle, Jesus slept.

"Imagine," my mother would tell her friends, "Soledad hadn't thought of this. *¡Que bruta! ¿Verdad?*"

When my mother told my father she was going to give birth to a child who might look like him, he laughed all the way to the cantina and got drunk on tequila. Later my mother would tell me that my father was a *borracho*, a good-for-nothing man.

"Why did you marry him?" I would challenge.

"I don't know," she would snap at me.

Another tale the white society ladies liked to hear was how my mother had considered returning to her hometown in Jiquilpan to dig a hole, squat Indian style, and deliver me.

"And what would you have done after Letty was born?" some one would ask, eyeing me as I walked away with the coffee pot. (I might have poured hot coffee on their pretty silk dresses if they had asked while I was serving them.)

"Yes, and what would you have done with Letty?" Aunt Luisa would ask, shuffling the canasta cards as the other ladies got ready for a new game.

"Notify the nuns where to find Letty so they would have to figure out what to do with her. If an Indian couple found her before the nuns did, better yet. They would raise her as family."

"What if I had died?" I asked my mother once when I had grown immune to her jokes. She replied as arrogantly as ever, "Well, the day I spoke to God personally, I would have explained why I didn't want to have a dark-skinned child, much less a daughter who doesn't appreciate how it is to live like decent people." I think I cried once or twice over this, but that was all.

Secretly, I wished an Indian couple had found me. Then I would be at the marketplace selling vegetables, or making nice warm tortillas and eating them with lots of chiles. Perhaps I would been taught a trade—I might have become a potter or a weaver. Or I might have become a fat baby with a round face suckling on my Indian mamma's breast. Oh, how I envied children wrapped in their mammas' *rebozos* each time I went to the supermarket. I would have preferred being of those children, wearing *huaraches* and sucking my thumb, snot on my nose. Or I may have become a Huichole shaman and be recognized for my wisdom. Instead I was cooped up at home ironing my brothers' shirts or my stepfather's pants. Today I know the real reasons my mother didn't move back to her family home and abandon me to the countryside.

One, the household in which she had once lived as a spoiled, white lady had been sold to developers and her parents had moved to Mexico City. Also, my mother had to think about Bonita, "Beauty," her precious *guerita* with light brown hair and blue eyes, five years older than me. She wouldn't want to live in the country and grow up among chickens, cows, goats, and pigs. Bonita was a "born lady," like my mother, and my mother wanted her to remain in Guadalajara to give her the best Catholic-school education. Bonita had lots of friends her own age and of the same social class who always had time to play games. When I was Bonita's age, my friends were the servants' daughters, children they hid from my mother so they wouldn't be fired.

Later in life my mother repented this tyranny. She took it upon herself to educate all the servants' boys (not the girls) who were born out of wedlock, regardless of their color. She would spend her grocery money buying uniforms for the boys and see to it that their mothers registered them in school. She stopped when Georgina, my Aunt Luisa's favorite maid, accused my mother of wanting to kidnap her son. "No," my mother replied in her defense, "I just want the boys to get an education because they are men." Smiling she would go on. "Men, no matter what, will always get ahead."

What my mother didn't know was that one day I would be a writer and tell this story.

Victoria Alegria Rosales is a San Francisco poet and was born in Mexico; She is currently teaching and working on her M.F.A. at San Diego State University.

Rita Arditti (right) with sister, 1938

But You Don't Look Jewish

Rita Arditti

Recently I had a conversation with an Ashkenazi Jewish couple about the Palestinian uprising and the Israeli government's response to it. The Israeli government is overwhelmingly composed of Ashkenazi Jews, though the majority of the population is not Ashkenazim. Some of my critical comments about Israel were not well received. They looked me straight in the eye and stated forcefully that whenever wrong things happen, Jews are blamed for them. Not wanting an argument, I retreated into silence for a moment. Then, almost casually, I mentioned that I was a Sephardic Jew and that my family also had relatives living in Israel. Immediately, the mood of the conversation changed. Now, in a friendly manner, they asked questions regarding my cultural background and personal history. My previous comments were no longer seen as anti-Semitic.

I left that conversation with mixed feelings: glad that we had reached a more meaningful level of communication, but once again reminded that most people—Jews and non-Jews—are often totally oblivious to the existence of the Sephardim.

I started to explore my origins twelve years ago. I was motivated by a gnawing sense of "differentness" I felt in the company of Ashkenazi Jews—both in Argentina and in the United States. I could not understand why I felt so different from other middle-class Jews, and in the beginning I attributed this feeling to personal idiosyncrasies. When my attempts to sort out what I thought were just individual differences didn't provide an adequate explanation, I started reading about and reflecting on the different historical and cultural circumstances that had shaped my experience.

I grew up in a large, tight-knit Sephardic community in Argentina. I began to realize that part of my sense of self derives from Sephardic Jewish history, a history that shapes how I feel and how I interpret the world. By delving into the incredibly rich and exciting history of the Sephardim, I developed a keen sense of wonder about my heritage. The anger and pain that I had felt about my marginality started to go away.

Generally, accounts of Jewish history present the Sephardim as playing a minor and secondary role. Media presentations about the Holocaust don't mention Sephardic communities—such as Salonika in Greece or Bitola in Yugoslavia—that were destroyed, or of Sephardim survivors of the Holocaust. It was deeply moving to learn recently of a bust in Bitola of a Jewish partisan heroine, Estreya Ovadia, who perished fighting near the Yugoslav-Greek border. The image of a Sephardic female freedom fighter during World War II was totally new to me.

In the United States, Ashkenazi Jews have made their mark in the arts, in the professions, and in the sciences. Yiddish expressions have become part of the American culture (at least in places with large Ashkenazi populations) and Eastern European Jewish culture has been immortalized in Broadway musicals and Hollywood movies.

The invisibility of Sephardim in American history is ironic, as there are intimate connections between the two. The same day that Spanish Jews were forced to leave Spain—August 1, 1492—Christopher Columbus also left Spain. He had to use the port of Palos because the more convenient port of Cadiz was too crowded with hapless Jews praying that the expulsion order would be rescinded. It is a fact that Columbus's voyage would not have taken place without the influence and money of his *Converso* backers. (The *Conversos* were Jews who became Christians to avoid the horrors of the Inquisition; many continued to practice Judaism in secret.) Furthermore, his second trip was financed from confiscated Jewish property, including the sale of precious religious objects. Spanish Jews often acted as intellectual bridges, bringing technology and ideas from the Greeks and the Arabs into the Christian world that made his voyage possible.

The history of the Jewish community in the United States began with the arrival—by a fluke of history—of twenty-three Sephardic Jews in September 1654. These Jews came from Recife, Brazil, trying to escape the Inquisition, after the Dutch were defeated by the Portuguese. Expelled from Brazil, they set out for Holland in a convoy of sixteen ships. Fifteen of these ships arrived safely, but one was blown off course and captured by Spanish pirates. These Sephardim, held to be sold as slaves, were eventually rescued and taken to New Amsterdam.

The theme of expulsion is a central one in Sephardim culture. When, as a child, I asked: "Where did our family come from, and why do my relatives speak Ladino? (Ladino is the language of the Sephardim, which is fifteenth century Spanish with local words of the places where they went into exile and some Hebrew. It is also known as Judezmoor Judeo-Spanish.) The first explanation my parents offered was always the banishment from Spain. The expulsion was an ever-present theme in our lives, and the emotions connected with it were complex. Certainly part of the message was that exile was a common occurrence in Sephardic history, and that it could happen again. But there was also a sense of pride associated with our fortitude: our ancestors had been expelled because they refused to renounce their faith. They had been true to their origins and loyal to their culture. They were

Jews who would go to any extremes to maintain their Jewishness. We, their descendants, were expected to do the same, even if sometimes we could not articulate or agree on what that meant.

In addition to commitment and pride, hope and endurance were emotional qualities instilled in me by my Sephardim history. We left Spain hoping one day to be allowed back. The story goes that those who departed took the keys of their houses and passed these from parents to children, through generations, waiting for the day when the keys would be used to return to their homes. It is claimed that when some Jews went back after centuries, their keys still fit the doors of their houses.

The Sephardim always stress that Sephardic culture did not disappear. Though our ancestors integrated themselves successfully in many countries that received them, they kept their language, their music, and their traditions. This ability to endure and the refusal to blur differences has always been considered a strength and proof of resilience and integrity. These qualities—commitment, pride, endurance, and hope—that stem from our history have influenced me, and I recognize them as part of my emotional makeup. Particularly, the abilities to persist in difficult circumstances and to derive strength from a long-range perspective seem to be characteristics I have "inherited" from my background.

These qualities played a crucial role in helping me carve a life for myself substantially different from the one expected of me as a Sephardic woman. In my family, all the women were housewives and mothers. Only one of my mother's sisters, who was considered "peculiar," worked outside of the home. We, the daughters, were supposed to get married soon after high school, have children, and live our lives in the context of the Sephardic community. I still remember the puzzled look on my father's face when I announced that I planned to go to the university. When it became clear that I wanted a different life, I felt quite isolated from other Sephardim and fantasized that Ashkenazi women had an easier time moving into the wider world. This, undoubtedly, contributed to my sense of "differentness" from them.

One observation that I have made about the Sephardim that I have not been able to explain satisfactorily and that still amazes me is the following: the Sephardim have an uncanny, almost eerie, ability to recognize each other. After the expulsion, the Sephardim dispersed widely in many different countries (Holland, England, Turkey, Italy, Greece, and others), where they were exposed to many and varied cultural influences. However, Sephardim from different countries easily recognize each other with almost total certainty. I like to think that we have been so marginalized and fragmented, we developed special skills to help us survive, to find others like us and to reconnect.

Our collective memory has also played a central role in keeping us alive.

Historical memory is the antidote to invisibility. We have had to look back in time to get images that reinforce and help us understand our social identity. As an individual, looking for ways to connect with my background, especially while in therapy, I explored the memories of my childhood. Religious holidays with a large family, Sephardic foods, and Ladino sayings framed my childhood.

The power of language became clear to me when I realized that whole categories of experience and early recollections could be suddenly awakened by hearing Ladino. Ladino is a very expressive and genteel language; just a few words of Ladino could bring back scenes, memories, and moods that I had completely forgotten.

There are close to half a million Jews in Argentina; it is the fifth largest Jewish community in the world. The Sephardim community numbers between 70,000 and 90,000. Growing up in a Sephardic household, playing with numerous cousins and sisters, I did not meet non-Jewish and Ashkenazi children until I went to school. My early memories were completely embedded in Sephardic culture. When I first met an Ashkenazi Jewish girl at school, I did not believe she could be a Jew—and I know she felt the same about me.

My personal identity is rooted in my early history and in the identity of the group into which I was born. Only when I was able to make these connections could I understand some of the forces that had shaped my life and influenced my choices. For me, my Sephardic identity and my Jewish identity are one and the same.

Not being recognized as a Jew means I have often witnessed anti-Semitic statements "from the inside." When I protest and identify myself as a Jew, I am often told that I am "different" from those "penny-pinching Jews" with Russian-sounding names who are the real Jews.

And indeed, when I married an Ashkenazi Jew, I did feel that I was becoming more "legitimate" as a Jew and that I had gone a step up in the ladder of Jewishness. I could well understand the experience of the Sephardic woman I met on a trip to Israel, who told me that her family had been in Israel for centuries and spoke both Ladino and Hebrew, but who felt she needed to learn Yiddish in order to feel like a real Jew!

When I identify myself as a Sephardic Jew, I want people to know my background and to appreciate the particular characteristics that have been essential to the survival of the Sephardim. One of these is the ability to move between cultures and to have practical strategies for living within different communities.

To deny our history is to obliterate an incredibly important part of the Jewish experience and to collude with the stereotyped assumptions that are made about us. The lack of Sephardic Jewish images in mainstream and in U.S. Jewish culture contributes to our invisibility. There are only 150,000 Sephardim in the United States, primarily in New York, Los Angeles, Seattle, and Atlanta. As a result, it is fairly easy to forget our existence.

I like to think that the worldliness that the history of the Sephardim exemplifies could help break barriers between Jews and non-Jews. Maintaining one's history and traditions while allowing for enrichment from other cultures can help to create a world where sectarianism does not thrive. This seems, in our times, an absolutely essential quality to ensure that humankind will have a future.

I was born in Argentina in a middle-class Sephardic Jewish family. My ancestors were expelled from Spain in the fifteenth century when Spain became a Catholic country again; they ultimately settled in Turkey. Both my parents were Turkish Jews who had grown up speaking fifteenth-century Spanish, or as we call it, "Español Antiguo" (Old Spanish) or Ladino.

I have never thought of myself as a woman of color until I immigrated to the United States in 1965. Because of my accent, my Mediterranean looks, and my place of birth, often I have been treated like a person of color, that is, in a patronizing, derogatory way. My middle-class upbringing and my education (I have a doctoral degree in biology) have helped me survive economically in this society, but in everyday life (going to the supermarket, dealing with the utilities companies, getting a haircut, etc.) I have felt the brunt of racism.

I had mixed feelings about being part of this anthology (Will people think I am trying to claim a "woman of color" identity? Do I really fit?), but after two conversations with Elena Featherston, I realized that she understood the complexities of my situation. I trust the readers will make up their own minds about the usefulness of my article (originally written for a book on Jewish women and therapy) in this collection.

—**Rita Arditti**, *Cambridge, Massachusetts*

Saundra Sharp with her mother, 1954

Growing Up Integrated

Saundra Sharp

Two images fill my mind when I think about "growing up integrated." One is picketing the Woolworth five-and-dime stores in Cleveland in the mid-1950s. I was excited, scared, and surprised to see white people on the line with us. Outwardly I showed my indignation, but inside I secretly hoped that if any trouble broke out the white folks would remember that I was just a child and have some mercy.

The other image was less complicated (I thought then) but has had a much stronger effect. I was shopping at Halle's Department Store, the downtown upscale white store. We always got dressed up in clothes reserved for going to church to go shopping *downtown*. My patent leather shoes glowed, and my mother inspected my ears and my little white gloves to be sure they were clean. The most important thing, more than finding what we wanted, was to let the white folks know as soon as they saw us that we were okay—meaning we were clean enough to try on the clothes. Some of the sales ladies recognized my mother for what she was—a classy lady who could discuss Elizabethan literature with the best of them but right now was bent on getting the most out of this sale. Other clerks would follow us around suspiciously, not speaking, not letting us out of their sight. I always *felt* like a thief. I was a neon sign upholding the rightness of my being there, with every movement calculated to show that I was not stealing. And God forbid they should catch a Negro thief wearing black patent leather Mary Janes and white cotton gloves! Would that mean that the rest of us couldn't come downtown anymore? To this day I hate shopping!

The social pressures for integration also fostered around my house two groups of Negroes: us and "Those Negroes Over There." "Those Negroes" had their hair "conked," drank wine on corners, sassed whites, appeared unemployed, and were generally too loud. I was given to understand that white people didn't like them at all. By implication that meant white folks liked us *some*. There were also two groups of whites: the bad ones who were responsible for all this mess in the first place and the good ones my grandmother worked for as a domestic.

The timeline for growing up integrated in the South was *Brown vs. Board of Education of Topeka* decision in 1954 that declared segregation in public schools unconstitutional; the Montgomery Bus Boycott; and the murder of Civil Rights activist Emmett Till. The "white only" signs were coming down, but the Klan was growing up, and those rosy-cheeked youngsters who sat on their fathers' shoulder taking in a picnic-style lynching were now sitting in Congress or on the boards of agencies that bent the shoulders of our fathers.

In the North, there was a "first Negro" in every office; property redlining was being challenged; young men were turning an alphabet letter into a last name; and every Monday we stopped eating dinner to watch Nat King Cole on television. Everywhere, going to church was a lot more interesting; the devil was named Jim Crow, the angel Gabriel was Martin Luther King, and Jesus was on the verge of becoming colored. It was all termed "progress," but blacks could still be beaten...to death.

As a daughter from above the Mason-Dixon line, I was sheltered from the harsh realities of racism. Like most northern cities in the 1950s, Cleveland had no signs posted. You had to figure out where you didn't belong, and middle-class parents tended to do that *for* their children to avoid having to explain.

I came home from nursery school one day in tears because my classmate, Mary, had torn up the picture I made to bring to Mommy. Mary had also, I threw in as an afterthought, called me a name. I was more distressed about the drawing.

The following day, when my mother dropped me off at the nursery, she lingered a bit until she had identified Mary. "Are you the one who tore up my little girl's drawing yesterday?" my mother asked quietly. The curly-blond, blue-eyed doll stared intently at my mother, nodding yes. "And did you call her a name?" She nodded again. "What name?" "A nigger," Mary pronounced innocently. Heads spun. "Do you know what a nigger is?" my mother asked. "Unh-unh," Mary responded. "A nigger, said my mother, "is a little girl who tears up another little girl's drawing. Now what does that make you?" The nursery director moved to intercept, too late. "A nigger," pronounced Mary, with complete acceptance. "Yes," my mother said sweetly. Then she rose and floated out of the nursery, leaving a trail of dumbstruck adults. That was my first time being called a nigger, and my first lesson in handling racism.

By adolescence I recognized that there was something dangerous yet intangible out there, and a fierce amount of energy was being exerted to protect me from "it." (My virginity was also an unmentioned, and I actively protected "it" and sometimes wondered if the two had been confused or blended.) Kids my age were facing what looked like the entire U.S. Army outside Central High School in Little Rock, Arkansas. We cheered and prayed for them, but privately I wondered what was so bad about their old school that they were willing to go through this?

There is a difference between desegregation and integration. Psychologist Na'im Akbar, a professor at Florida State University states, "In the past the schools, the church, the neighborhood itself supported the development of the black child. The negative side of the integration coin is that it wasn't integration, but rather desegregation which served as an instrument that destroyed that support system, and we were left only with the *opportunity* to *assimilate*." Film programer and teacher Cheryl Chisolm experienced this. In 1960, she was thrust from segregation into an Atlanta prep school where blacks made up 1 percent of the population. "What I meant by integration was not what white people meant," she explains. "White people thought it meant us becoming honorary whites."

Those of us who represent the first generation to live without any public manifestations of segregation did not create the integration dream. It was our *parent's* program. They were the generals, designing the dream. We were the footsoldiers sent into the field to see if it was real, or could be made real. We were drilled, grilled, rehearsed, preached at, prayed over, and propagandized into facial fitness! Some became casualties even before reaching the enemy, which is why we can look back and ask the seemingly arrogant question, "Did Momma do the right thing?…And what might have been the alternative actions?"

A black statesman once said something to the effect that we were so busy getting on the train that we never asked where it was going. It seemed about to split rails. In my community we were taught that we were better than white people, no matter what they said or did to us. Then, as we neared our entry into the white domain, we were told that we would have to work hard in school, on the job to prove that we were just as good as they were. If I was already better, then why did I have to prove anything? And if they weren't going to let me into their corporate office, trust me at their cash register, or let me fly their airplane, then how could I be considered better? It was a contradiction not to be discussed. Rather, it was submerged in that lifting finger under the chin, "And keep your head up, you hear?!" Then a weighty, "Be careful." Just be careful.

I played my part, and I was good. I never dropped the banner of the race by being too loud, using "ain't," losing my temper, or failing to smile politely. I minded my p's and q's and kept my head up while trying not to appear "saddity" (remember that one?) around my peers. But I was never, never at ease. In his introduction to *The Price of the Ticket*, the late James Baldwin states, "Not only was I not born to be a slave; I was not born to hope to become the equal of the slave-master." Jimmy, where were you when I needed you?

Interestingly, despite the push all around for integration and our success at it, nobody in my crowd brought white friends to parties, or bike riding, or to the neighborhood pool. We weren't interested in creating our own experiments. It was a natural discrimination that said in a positive way that it was all right for us to be ourselves with ourselves. This was real; everything else was just a game plan.

Peggy Dammond Preacely, an advertising executive, feels that her parents made all the right choices. From the age of two through the fourth grade she attended The Modern School in Harlem, a black-owned private elementary school that still caters to the middle-class black family. Then the exclusive and affluent Dalton School on Manhattan's East Side opened its radical arms to bring some of Harlem's promise into the Dalton aristocracy on scholarship. Peggy and her brother Hank, writer Samuel Delaney, and District of Columbia Judge Judith Wilson were among some twenty students of varying ages who found themselves rubbing shoulders with Alger Hiss's son, playwright William Saroyan's daughter, and the Nina Rosenwalds of the world.

"I felt the pressure," Peggy recalls, "but I also felt like I was on a crusade and loved it." Part of the pressure was needing to show that black kids could keep up with white kids. But she had some unusual advantages. Her great uncle was the militant William Monroe Trotter, publisher of Boston's *Guardian* newspaper for more than thirty years. In the family tradition, Peggy's mother taught her Afro-American history at night. "So when the white kids said something in error, I'd stand up and say, 'That's not true!' Sometimes they stared, sometimes they guffawed. I'd be nervous, but I was 'carrying the banner.' I wore it in the classroom, on the basketball court, at dances. I was very careful who I brought there as a date because it had to be someone who could talk to these people."

Outside school, the students learned to switch worlds with the snap of a finger. "We learned to speak two languages every day," Peggy continues. "On the bus going home from school we spoke to whites in their language. Soon as we crossed 96th Street going uptown, we changed back to street language so no one from the neighborhood would think we were being uppity. I went to the Harlem Y for activities. Sometimes we'd pass for Puerto Rican. It was a schizophrenic existence, but we didn't think of that at the time."

We also forgot to ask or even estimate what the train ticket costs. Dr. Akbar observes that "There was so much pressure to accept that integration was wonderful—our parents told us it was, our leaders told us it was when it wasn't; there was a strong tendency to deny the pain."

Somewhat reluctantly, Preacely recalls how color was on and under everything. She was almost the same shade as some of her white classmates. "You're not really Negro," they would say, and I'd be trying to explain. I was concerned that I couldn't be black enough. I remember, at one point around the fifth grade, I didn't want my mom to come to school because she was browner than me and that would raise more questions, and I was just tired of dealing with it."

Other benign attitudes started to change when the children became teens and dating entered the picture. The girls could handle the drop in social invitation, the new snubs. But for Hank Dammond it was the glory of attention, received through a barbed wire.

"My brother had some difficult experiences," Peggy says. "He was a male; he was the one who was going to *date* these women. It was a social thing, and the social pressure was terrible. Eventually he withdrew and went back to a black public school. My parents were stunned." Stunned because they didn't think they had sent their children to Dalton just to be integrated, but to receive an excellent education.

Still, Peggy Preacely feels positive about her Dalton days. "Because of that experience I can deal in any society at any time, and I'm comfortable everywhere. It's also because of my parents' attitude. We were cash poor, but we were culturally and family wealthy."

Hank had retreated. But a number of brothers being dropped into white society with a natural curiosity stimulated by the look-but-don't-touch rule were pushed across the color line. An associate remembers looking from his new white bride to his mother and thinking, "Is this what you meant, Mom? Am I doing the right thing? Is this enough?"

"I had more trouble with the black middle-class than I ever had with white racists!" remarks Robert Earl Price, a writer raised in, and returned to, Atlanta, Georgia, where he remembers a childhood among so many blacks that he could go for weeks without seeing a white person.

"The black middle-class tried to stamp out any sign of rebellion. All boys in the South were taught to hold their peace because every interaction with whites was considered an opportunity." For his elementary education, Robert's mother, an army nurse, chose an all-black Catholic school where all the teachers were white nuns. "The message we got," says Robert, " is that white teachers gave a better education than blacks. This left little room to protest negative ideas that were racially motivated."

To compensate for not having a black Catholic high school, boys were sent to an integrated boy's club on Saturdays. Robert remembers, "All would be going well until there was something missing. Then they would bring in all the black boys and interrogate us, because it was understood that being black we stole. After a while I stopped going, but I would tell my mother I went, because I didn't want the headaches. Also, after a while some of the bloods did start to steal because they had learned it was expected of them."

Jean Collins's family was part of a group of Mississippians who followed a rumor of employment all the way to Iowa. The segregated life moved with them to the town of Waterloo. When she reached the sixth grade, Jean and her younger sister were invited to integrate by themselves the Roosevelt Elementary School, a school of several hundred white children. They were promised protection; by recess the first day, Jean had already given up one front tooth to the welcoming committee, and she still had a lot to learn.

"We had one [Asian] and one Jewish family in our neighborhood," she recalls. "There was no interaction between blacks and whites, so I didn't know that the whole thing of white-Negro was a skin color. What I remember most is that a lot of the kids would tell 'colored' jokes. One of my new little friends noticed I wasn't reacting so she asked, 'Aren't you colored?' I answered, 'No, I don't think so. What are you?' 'White,' she replied. And I said, 'Well, then I am, too.'"

Dr. Akbar notes that, "The wording of the 1954 Supreme Court decision says, in essence, that segregated schools are damaging to black children and what they really need is to be in school with white children. This is the message our parents heard. Nowhere does the decision say that segregated schools are damaging to white children. This omission suggests that we have nothing of value to bring with us."

Even some who knew their value suffered damage to the psyche, despite the best efforts of parents. How stunned I was the day I realized that in my dreams I saw myself as being white. I came to this realization during the seventies when I was busy being very black, and the discovery was humiliating. Worse, I was certain I was the only black person in America with this counter-revolutionary problem. But Dr. Richard D. King, a San Francisco–based psychiatrist, attests to the fact that the experience is widespread. "It's called a shadow," King states. "A part of myself that is very different than what I am, but is very much like what society wants everyone to be. The standard is a white one, and the need is to be some kind of white person to gain acceptance. This includes identifying with white images."

The experience is not only widespread, its source is deliberate, like society painting white heros in glowing colors but praising black heroes only if they're in some subservient category."

Jean Collins also found herself with a blond-haired, blue-eyed female in place of her own image. She states, "It was then that I knew that I'd given away too much for an empty dream, an empty promise. So I started to fight back, to regain my identity."

Fighting back. All those integrated babies, grown up and filled with an urgency to take things into our own hands. Preacely, at nineteen, went South to work in the voter registration program. She learned how to pick cotton and became very familiar with southwest Georgia jails. Years later, concerned parents in Boston developed the Freedom School concept around her kitchen table. Cheryl Chisolm volunteered as a teacher at the first Boston Freedom School.

Price was part of the Student Non-Violent Coordinating Committee and uses his writing talent as a political tool, believing that "theatre allows people to rehearse for change." (His play, *Black Cat Bones for Seven Sons* is currently running in Atlanta.) The Wilmington 10 Defense Committee caught my energy, and I campaigned for Mayor Kenneth Gibson in Newark even though I lived in New York. Collins, a writer and editor, was managing editor for the University of Wisconsin's prestigious magazine, *Arts In Society,* and the first black on the art department staff. But in 1978 she brought charges against the university for discrimination. We grew up not only to flesh out the dream but to demand that it be made real.

As summarized by Julian Bond in the introduction to *Eyes On the Prize,* the "essential prize" was *freedom* and the struggle was to provide "*choices for black people.*" For the lay people who didn't have a lot of information to work with, the prize and the dream was very American: a nicer home in a better neighborhood and something more for your kids than you had for yourself. Integration, and with it assimilation, appeared to be one of the main paths to freedom.

But what do you pack when you purse a dream? And what do you leave behind? The present generation of parents have come to meet the train.

In Denver, a mother of teens seeks a counselor's help because her daughter doesn't want to be associated with anything black. In Detroit, a woman who dealt with integration by raising her children as nationalists preparing for "the revolution" and sent her son to high school in Africa, watches painfully as he selects a white woman to be the mother of his children. She wonders if he simply O.D.'d on blackness, or is it the force of the times? In Los Angeles, a distressed mother comes into the black-oriented bookshop for something, *anything* for her three-year-old who has just rejected a black doll. The little girl, who is the only black in her nursery school, rejected the image with the pronouncement, "I'm not black, I'm white!"

Is this where the train was going?

Is this how much the ticket costs?

Robert Price observed, "After they get through doing whatever they are going to do with Jesse—which is not to make him president—then maybe our people will see that the process is going to have to be altered so that we coexist on the planet while retaining our ethnicity. Author John Oliver Killens always taught us, 'To be universal is to be very specific.' Those strengths that are uniquely ours we *infuse* into the culture in a way that enhances the culture and also our struggle."

But "our struggle" brings a blank face and a question mark from those we deemed to be our future. I was about to initiate a somewhat political discussion with one of Hollywood's rising black directors, when the man's son walked by—a charismatic seven-year-old, dressed in a Rambo T-shirt, with a Rambo headband wrapped around his jeri-kurl, carrying a two-foot Rambo toy gun. In a flash I understood that I could not hold the conversation I had planned with someone who felt comfortable cloning his beautiful black child into a mini-Rambo.

We are pushing onward to the primary goal of integration, and all the Howard Beaches and all the Forsythe Counties scattered across America don't seem to be bringing us home again.

So the question may not be "Did Momma do the right thing?" but rather, "Did she do it too well?"

Saundra Sharp is an Los Angeles-based writer, poet, and filmmaker.

We, Black and Indian women, are told that our unaccounted for mistreatment at the hands of white men is a figment of our imaginations… Some of the people expressing negative opinions about the value of Black people and Indian people talking together are neither Indian or Black, so what is their role in this issue?

— Marion E. Douglas, "On the Occasion of the
Quincentennial of the Columbus (Mis)Adventure"
(*The Circle*, 1992)

Cheng Imm Tan (right) and sister

Thinking about Asian Oppression and Liberation

Cheng Imm Tan

I was nine years old during the 1967 race riots in Malaysia. There were gruesome stories of Chinese who were killed. There were twenty-four-hour curfews. The streets were deathly quiet. We huddled to listen to the news, anxiously wondering how near the riots were to our home, wondering how many more had been killed, wondering if the rest of the family in other towns were safe.

For as long as I could remember, we were careful. We always had to watch what we said and what we did. We were always very careful not to bring too much attention on ourselves. I remember the huge fight I had with my whole family when I wrote a letter to the minister of education responding to his invitation to critique the educational system. My parents were sure that if I sent it we would all end up in jail.

In Malaysia, at least, I knew ethnic conflicts existed. I knew what to look out for, what to do, what to avoid, how to be. As an immigrant Asian woman, particularly when I first came to America in 1971, there were no road maps to help navigate my way through U.S. color racism. In many ways it was a new game with new rules, and I did not know how to play. Asians, like other immigrants, come to the United States filled with hopes and dreams, many escaping the terrors of war, others seeking the "better life" that eludes them in their own country due to internal and international politics and economics.

After fourteen years in the United States, I'm just beginning to understand and to be able to name what is going on. And every day I see other Asians continue to struggle in confusion, trying to make sense of their experience.

Although our political and historical realities are very different, many Asian groups share similar experiences and overlapping histories, as well as cultural and religious philosophies and perspectives. In addition, we have all experienced internal totalitarian oppression, feudalism, colonialism, and racism.

Asian oppression has at least two layers. As Asians living in our countries of ethnic origin, we face the pressure of oppression that exists within them. Many behaviors that mystify people outside our cultures originate in response to totalitarian regimes and abuses faced by us in our own countries and cultures.

As immigrants and as people of color, there is another layer of persecution imposed historically from Western colonialism, and presently from capitalistic economic imperialism and racism. Asian liberation means not only freedom from outside racist abuse, but it also means getting rid of rigid cultural socialization patterns, passed down from generation to generation, that inhibit the expression of our full humanity/humanness.

These are some Chinese patterns I have been able to identify. Other Asians and people of color may find additional points of identification with them as well.

Isolation and self-reliance. Depend on yourself. Don't expect any outside help, except from the immediate family—and sometimes not even from them. Pretend to be "making it" even when you are not. The more owning class you are, the more shameful it is to ask for help.

Trust no one. If you read Chinese history (and probably other Asian history as well) or watch Chinese movies, there is so much chaos, so much intrigue and oppression from warlords, invasions, and counter-revolutions that it is difficult to know whom to trust or what the future will be like. Therefore, no one can be trusted. On the other hand, once one earns another's trust, the loyalty is for a lifetime.

Everything is fine. Even if it is not, say that it is. Silent, stoic forbearance is a valued virtue. You feel powerlessness to change things. The best you can do is to bear it. This has been crucial to Asian survival. Within a system, where authority is paramount, any act of protest, lack of cooperation, and even a sign of internal/personal dissatisfaction or disagreement could mean criticism, punishment, and or even death.

Be nice, be invisible. Don't show your true feelings. Don't show that you *have* feelings. Go with the majority. Don't offend or upset anyone. Don't question authority. Be nice all the time.

You have to be perfect. Perfection is valued *and* expected. Mistakes are not taken kindly—in the days of authoritarian warlords, people could be killed for the smallest mistake. In Japanese history, internalized self-criticism was so strong that suicide to redeem one's honor was considered acceptable and even encouraged. Thus, internalized self-criticism is as strong as society's.

Urgency. Never relax or let your guard down. Every minute is precious. There is no time to waste. Your survival and that of your family and your community may depend on taking advantage of every opportunity you encounter. There is no sense that you can shape your own destiny or have control of your own life.

Take nothing for granted. Be grateful for what you have and what you can get. Life is so unpredictable and insecure that you should be thankful simply to be alive.

Don't wash your dirty laundry in public. What happens in the family happens in the family. You don't let outsiders know about the struggles within your family or community; they might look down on you or use the information against you.

Don't show affection. If you love someone, don't tell him or her directly. Show your love by criticizing or putting pressure on them. Criticism and nagging are important to get your loved ones trained to "do the right thing." It is believed that showing affection to your kids means spoiling them; and later in life they will not be tough enough to take care of themselves.

Be prepared. The work ethic is strong. Save as much money as you can—you never know when you may need it. (In the old days your family's life might depend on being able to pay someone off.) It is better to postpone gratification and prepare for the emergencies of tomorrow.

Criticism, distrust, and competition. Compare yourself and your family to others in the community. Then criticize yourself and especially your children for not doing better. Push yourself and your loved ones to compete with relatives and neighbors. Who is earning more? Who has a bigger house? Who has smarter kids? Criticize constantly. This is insidious because it keeps us isolated.

Humiliation. Shame and humiliation are like death itself. Often children are punished by humiliating them in front of others. Public reprimands for mistakes are terrible. It not only affects the individual, but shames the entire family as well. Public shaming is a very effective tyranny.

Education for survival. The only way to get ahead is through study. I'm sure this comes from the Imperial exams which were the great equalizer in Chinese history. Even peasants could attain high government posts if they did well in the public Imperial exams. Today this pattern is ascribed to many Asians, especially immigrants, who have few connections.

Strong sense of community. The survival of the family, or the community, takes precedence over the survival of the individual. Put yourself last, your own needs are unimportant.

Don't toot your own horn. Your own needs are unimportant. Always put yourself down. If someone gives you a compliment, know that you are unworthy of it, be humble. Put everyone else first, and don't make trouble. Don't ask, give instead. Give and you will receive.

Women are not valued. In many Asian communities, girl children are not desired and not valued. Women are considered temporary family members, and when they marry they belong to their husband's family. Under Confucian ethic, women are instructed to obey their fathers as daughters, their husbands as wives, and eldest sons as widows. They had no identity of their own. The only time a woman is celebrated and praised is when she gives birth to a son. More than anyone else, a woman is expected to put herself last, to accept whatever comes her way with stoic endurance.

Direct communication of desires or conflicts is rude. Don't ask for things. Don't confront someone if you have disagreement. Instead, hint or imply or show by your actions that you are displeased. Other people are supposed to pick up these signals and figure the problem out by themselves. Historically, indirect communication was essential to survival in the face of oppression.

Insignificance. Despite rich histories and cultures we often feel insignificant because most of us have been colonized and have internalized a sense of inferiority. In addition, our cultures and arts are often appropriated in a superficial manner rather than being understood, celebrated, and valued.

Most of these behaviors are survival adaptations that allowed our ancestors to cope with the terror and insecurity of totalitarian feudal oppression. They have been incorporated into our way of life and have become identified as "cultural" patterns. In a racist world, when these patterns are seen as merely cultural, there is the implication that we and our cultures are defective and inferior. In addition, in a racist society any behavior that does not conform to its "norm" is seen as weird, dysfunctional, and "less than." Many of us have internalized this blame.

For immigrant Asians in America, random violence and terror are real. Despite the magnitude of our contributions, Asians are still considered outsiders. The history of the Asian experience in America documents exploitation, discrimination, and dehumanization. When times get hard, Asians are blamed, beaten, killed. We all "look alike"; we are all "gooks," "chinks," or something. We are often told to "go home." Hate crimes against Asians are disproportionately high relative to our population. A recent study showed that Asians are the number-one targeted group for hate crimes in America. So is it any safer here than in the countries that we fled?

U.S. racism is quite distinct. It is a color racism that affects all people of color, but this is not acknowledged. In the United States, racism against Asians isn't supposed to exist. Racism is recognized mainly in Black-White terms. Racism against Blacks is well documented and publicly acknowledged. However, the overriding message is that Asians are not oppressed. We are the successful "model minority." We were portrayed as "making it." The dubious indicators used to measure our success are inaccurate and loaded.

The primary goal of the model-minority thesis is to obscure the realities of racism. It is a thesis invented on the heels of the civil rights movement and at the height of Black activism. The argument that Asian cultural values and hard work are the keys to success was made as an indictment of other communities of color, and to advance the impression that the United States was a fair society that judged and rewarded people on merit, not by the color of their skin. Racism, according to this thesis, is not the real obstacle to the advancement of people of color. It serves not only to make Asian oppression invisible, but pits Asians against people of color, particularly Blacks.

The model-minority assertion holds up the success of a few to obscure the reality that most Asians in the United States are poor and struggling. It also conceals the suffering endured by those who "made it." In reality "making it" is often the result of *years* of hardship and strife, in low-paying, labor-intensive, and exploitative jobs and through generations of shared family sacrifice. Because racism against Asians is not publicly acknowledged and addressed, there is no context, language, or framework within which to place our experiences. We know something is wrong, but we cannot name it. We internalize the idea that something is wrong with us.

Daily, my Asian colleagues and I, who work with Asian battered women, fight some system or person, trying to get Asian women fair treatment or merely the services they have a right to but can't access because of language and cultural barriers. Every day, I see Asian women treated with disrespect, ignored, or overlooked because we speak with an accent. Every day, I see and meet Asians scared to speak up, scared to reach out, scared to even leave their homes. Too often I see Asians "punished" because they cannot quite conform to the expectations of white America: losing their children to state custody because they could not learn Western parenting skills fast enough, discrimination on jobs, or in housing. Our experience is like that of other people of color, except it is hidden.

Our isolation from other groups of color is also encouraged and maintained. Lies about other groups of color have been imposed on Asians— through the media and even the U.S. State Department—even before they get to this country. The misinformation, combined with language barriers and lack of accurate information about the intracacies of U.S. racism, has often resulted in the ease in which Asians are pitted against and isolated from other communities of color. It has set up painful, unnatural separations and barriers to getting close to other members of our human family. It has obscured the reality of our inherent human connectedness.

Our intracommunal distrust, isolation, and competitiveness are encouraged because they are useful to white racism. After all, the more we engage in these behaviors, the less effective we are in forming a united front to work toward change.

As Asian Americans and Asian immigrants, both our humanness and our oppression have been concealed. Our reality is rarely alluded to, let alone confirmed. We live in a country where the way we see ourselves and the way we experience the world is seldom reflected in images we see or stories we read. We constantly have to translate information in order to have it make sense, or to apply it to our own experience. A big part of who we are is always being denied, because there is "no space," no understanding, no welcome of our differences. We are then expected to conform to established norms and rules of being and behaving that do not include ones that reflect who we really are.

We need to remember that we are more than one-half the world's population and that liberation of the world from every form of oppression is in our hands. We are inherently powerful. We are capable of making meaningful changes to make the world a better place for all people. Our leadership is essential in the world. Our participation in world liberation is crucial. We are significant. We have thousands of years of wisdom to contribute to human liberation. Because no oppression can be completely eliminated unless all oppression is eliminated, ending Asian oppression is crucial to building a world that supports the liberation and reemergence of all people.

Rev. Cheng Imm Tan—the associate minister at large, and director of the Asian Women's Project sponsored by the Unitarian Universalist Urban Ministry—is a fourth-generation Chinese immigrant from Malaysia.

The Prize

Brenda Bankhead

Ruby Fields tried to avoid going to her window that morning. She had avoided lifting that ruffled curtain again ever since the accident, but the singing had finally gotten to her and drawn her from the comfort of her warm sheets to the kitchen. Ruby stood shivering in bare feet, her arms wrapped tight around her chest, her hands drawing her robe as close as possible. Yes, her ears had heard right: there was singing going on at this hour on this day. Ruby knew right away it had to be Dora. The voice was high and as thin as crystal. A child's pure voice. But at six o'clock in the morning? A day before her sister's funeral?

Ruby moved as quietly as she could toward the window as if her ten-year-old niece could hear through walls. Her hand recoiled slightly from the cool linen feel of the curtain, but Ruby put her mind to it and pushed the ruffles away to reveal the yard behind her house.

Dora Reeds sat on the steps of the house behind Ruby's like a bird perched on a line. Her legs drawn up to her meager chest, she seemed to balance on the edge of the cement steps. Her face arched upward toward the early morning sky. Her eyes were closed.

Is she praying? Ruby thought. Is that it? But Ruby knew that it was not a prayer, or at least not a prayer of sorrow or penance that the girl was singing. There was too much joy in the song for it to be those things. Ruby wanted to swoon, to fall through darkness and touch the face of the Lord when she awoke. That's where her other niece was now. With God in heaven. Ruby looked at her remaining one and tried to feel pity, tried to feel something more than a logical concern, but she could not stop the image that leapt into her brain. If I was a rooster, she thought, you wouldn't be sitting on that porch, singin' like that. No, you would not be there at all. If I was a rooster, there would be blood.

Ruby went to her back door off the kitchen and opened it enough to poke her head through. The air was cold.

"Dora," Ruby hissed. "Dora!"

"What are you hissing about?" John said as he entered the room.

Ruby turned to face her younger brother. She thought: So you've stopped your crying. You've let your ol' big watery eyes finally dry up. About time.

"What are you doing up at this hour?" she asked him.

"I couldn't sleep. Same as you, I guess. I heard the singing, too, although it didn't wake me. I didn't sleep at all last night. I knew it had to be Dora," he said.

"You think I'm deaf? I want to know why. Why is she out there this time of morning? Huh? Tell me that?"

"I don't know," he said, "but I think you should let her be." He drew back the kitchen curtains now and looked out over the backyard.

"It isn't natural, " Ruby said. "Maybe we should take her to the doctor."

"There's no money or time for another doctor now," John said. It'll have to wait till after…"

"Something is definitely not right in that child's mind," Ruby said.

"Can you blame her?" John asked. "She stood there and watched her sister fall."

"But still…to be singing! Don't she got no sense!"

"There's no sense in it," John said, "no sense in it at all."

He continued to look out over the backyard at the girl on the steps. "She looks just like a little chick perched on the steps that way," he said. "Just like a little black chick."

And if I was a rooster, Ruby thought, there would be blood.

John suddenly pushed himself away from the sink and covered his face with his hands. "Oh, that was one beautiful child," he said, his voice breaking. "That hair! She got the good blood of the family all right! She would have been a fine woman. Fine." He began to sob and left the room.

You wouldn't think they were sisters at all, Ruby thought, but for that daddy of theirs. Still, the girls' daddy had been good to her niece Wilma, and he had reminded Ruby of her much-loved husband Jack. That had been a good man. Ruby Thoreau had been a young woman of twenty, living in Oklahoma, when she had met and married Jack Fields, a lean, hardworking farmhand. They had come to California, found jobs as domestics, and bought the property with the two houses on it. The thought of the children they would have…Ruby smiled at her memory of the one man she had ever loved, remembered how the yard out back had been green and lush under his care. He had loved flowering things so much. And he had loved Ruby. He had been gentle to her in the night and brought her robe to her in the morning when she had needed such tenderness. When he had died young of a heart attack, Ruby had thought she could not go on. She had been so full of heartache and anger at his leaving her, she had gone out and ripped up all the flowering things Jack had planted in the yard. She had felt she could not bear to see them without his smiling face and strong hands mixed among the colors and foliage. That had been thirty-two years ago, and Ruby had never replanted. She had thought about it from time to time but never seemed to get the energy to do it. She finally had the brown, gaping holes and the whole yard covered in cement when she let Wilma Reeds and her two daughters move in after their daddy had been killed in a car accident. Ruby had thought it would be easier to keep clean that way.

Remembering Jack and the happiness they had shared together made Ruby clutch the sill of the door she still leaned against. The horror of the last two days almost overwhelmed her, and she wanted to swoon again but she did not. She drew herself up and leaned further out the open door.

"Wilma!" she shrieked across the yard, "Wilma, come out here and get this girl off the porch!"

A bedroom window facing out toward the yard opened immediately. So, Ruby thought, the girl's mother had been listening, too.

"I can hear you," Wilma Reeds called. "You don't have to shout."

"Well, tell her to get in the house. Don't she have any sense at all? It's not decent."

"Ruby heard Wilma's harsh whisper to the girl clear across the yard.

"Dora, get your ass in here before I have to come out there and make you sorry. I don't need this today."

At the sight of her aunt's head protruding from the screen door, Dora Reeds started and clamped her mouth shut. Now she scrambled to her feet and scuttled inside the front door of her house, silently. Her dark, terry bathrobe trailed behind her like a shadow.

"Don't your mama have enough to worry about without you getting sick?" Ruby shot at the small figure.

A few hours later when Dora, her hair coiled and separated into geometric patterns on her head, stood before her aunt, Ruby could not help but think about the little girl's daddy again. Wilma had caused an uproar in the family when she had defied everyone and gone and married Martin Reeds, a very dark black man. A very, very dark black man and not good-looking at all. "Who would want to marry a man like that?" everyone had asked. No one in her family. The Thoreaus prided themselves on being Creole: Colored and French with some Cherokee thrown in. To marry someone beyond a certain caramel coloring was considered a betrayal to their good breeding, a wild seed in the lightly colored garden that had taken generations of selective choices to perfect. How can Wilma marry that black man? everyone said; we'll all be sorry when the children are born. When Janetta Reeds had been born two years later with white skin and light green eyes, everyone had been shocked, and a bit suspicious, too. You could never tell with that one, Ruby said to herself, thinking of Wilma, distraught and restless in the back house. But Janetta Reeds had grown enough to look like her father to allay any doubts about who had fathered her. When Dora had been born two years after Janetta, she had surprised no one. She looked exactly like Martin Reeds. She was lucky she had been born second. She was accepted much more easily in that position than if she had been born first. Her sister's narrow nose and light skin had been the prize, the brass ring the Thoreaus reached for in their merry-go-rounds of courtship, what they hoped for when they chose mates with sandy hair and light eyes. They didn't want to marry white but as close to it as possible—just that hint of colored was just fine. And Janetta Reeds had had two thick, dark auburn braids going down her back, and her family had loved her dearly for them. They had made her a heroine in everyone's eyes. Aunts and cousins, who had looked at Wilma during her first pregnancy as if she had done something dirty, later cooed and aahed over the little pink bundle she had presented to them. They had fingered Janetta's silky curls between cold fingers and marveled at her thin lips. As Janetta had grown older they had pointed her out to people and said, "That's my grandniece" or "That's my cousin. The Thoreaus are good-looking people." And bringing Wilma up from behind, they had said with pride, "This here's her mother." It was almost a convenience that the Thoreau women had such trouble with their men dying young.

Ruby looked at Dora. The girl's hair was freshly washed and rolled about her head like dark brown snails. When loose, her hair was a tightly kinking halo around her face. The girl stood leaning against Ruby's kitchen counter, her lips slightly poked out in petulance. Ruby sat on a high stool by the stove and looked out over the rim of her glasses at her.

"You better be glad I'm doing this for you, cause your mama sure won't do it," Ruby said.

The girl poked out her lips a little more and began to chew on the bottom one, drawing the chapped skin away from the flesh with her top teeth.

"You want to look nice tomorrow, don't you?" Ruby asked her.

Dora nodded. "Yes, Ma'am," she said.

"Then sit down and let me see what I can do," Ruby said.

Dora approached and lowered her bottom on the stool in front of her aunt. Ruby surveyed the child's head in front of her. Wilma had washed her daughter's hair that morning, then wound it in coils all around the little girl's head. Ruby undid the coils to see if there was any dampness near the scalp. She did not want any water turning to steam near the scalp when she pulled the hot pressing comb through Dora's hair. When she was satisfied that the hair was completely dry, Ruby threw a towel over Dora's shoulders, then she plunged her index finger and the finger next to it into the small jar of hair oil. She rubbed the glob of blue grease between her two calloused palms, then across the soft, dark mass of Dora's hair. She would begin at the back of the head, the base of the neck, and work her way up.

"Put your head down, Dora. Let me get to your kitchen back here."

The girl obeyed and Ruby felt the short hairs there. As Ruby worked she thought of this hard-edged song she had heard that morning. It was not one with which she was familiar. She wondered where Dora had picked it up but she hesitated in asking the child about it. She hesitated asking the child about anything. Ruby wanted to know what had brought those children up on that roof in the first place. She had no doubt that Janetta had been the ringleader. The child had such a wild streak that had been allowed to reign free for most of her life. But what had touched that wild imagination enough to bring it to that roof in the middle of the night?

Ruby reached for the metal comb on the open flame of the stove she sat by and rubbed it in a white dish towel. If the towel did not get singed, then she knew the comb was hot enough to straighten kinky hair but not hot enough to burn it. As Ruby brought the comb to Dora's head, she thought that to ask about the singing that morning was not such a risky thing after all.

"I heard you singing this morning," she said, careful to keep any kind of accusation out of her voice.

"Uh huh," Dora said, drowsily. Her aunt's fingers massaging her scalp always made her sleepy.

"What song was that you were singing? I never heard you singing that before. From school?" Ruby asked.

"No," Dora said, her head still bent, "I made it up I was so happy."

Ruby put the comb back over its flame. She could not hide the tone in her voice this time.

"What you got to sing about?" she asked. "What you got to be happy about?"

"It was the sky," Dora said, "the sky was so beautiful this morning, Aunt Ruby."

Ruby's back became much straighter.

"Keep your head down, Dora. How many times I got to tell you that?" She pushed the girl's head down so that Dora's chin rested on her collarbone. Ruby felt Dora's muscles tighten.

"Don't get tense on me, now," she said. "You know I can't do these naps when you're as stiff as a board. Loosen up!" She grabbed the small, brown arms in front of her below the shoulders and shook them so that they flopped in Dora's lap.

Ruby reached for the comb again and rubbed it in the towel. The comb came away from the towel, smoking. Ruby looked at the brown burn on the towel, then she did a thing that she didn't think herself capable of. Bracing one hand against Dora's head, she brought the smoking comb to the short hairs in the naps of the girl's neck. The hair crackled and withered up in the path of the metal heat passing through it. The smell of burnt hair began to fill the kitchen. When she had brought the comb to the broken ends of its journey, Ruby let the back of the hot comb fall onto her niece's neck and rest there.

Dora's whole body jerked up in the chair as if she had been electrocuted. She began to shriek in short, high yelps. Ruby jerked her hand up, as if the same shock had passed through her own body and threw the straightening comb clattering across the top of the stove. She jumped up and ran to bathroom for the salve that they used for burns. She felt as though she was running through a tunnel, tight walls and darkness closing in around her. At the end of the tunnel Ruby saw a vision, which was in fact a memory— her memory of what had happened the night Janetta Reeds had fallen and slipped so neatly between the spaces of this world and into the next.

Something had drawn Ruby's eyes away from the dishes she had been washing that night. It had to have been something unheard for the girls had made no noise upon the roof. As Ruby had drawn the frilly blue-and-white curtain away from the window, she had gasped. The mixture of the clouds and the light from the moon had seemed to make the house beneath the girls disappear. With their white nightgowns billowing out around them, the children had been transformed into two small, fluttering ghosts hovering high above ground. Even then Ruby had sensed the first misstep in the dark, had seen the change in the fluttering waves of one nightgown as something brushed violently in front of it. The movement was too harsh and swift to be the breeze that had been blowing then. It was more ballooned, like the useless flailing of a person drowning, or a person falling, but she could not tell which one. Even when the falling girl had cried out, Ruby had not been able to tell if it was Dora or Janetta, and Ruby Fields, in her turn, had screamed out her husband's name as if he could turn concrete into soft, black earth.

Brenda Bankhead *is a Black woman writer born and raised in Los Angeles. Her work has appeared in* Obsidian II, Black Literature in Review, *and in various anthologies including* The World Between Women *(Herbooks) and* The Time of Our Lives *(Crossing Press).*

Early in the slave trade, Afrikan-Americans valued lighter skin because it was an economic and social commodity. It could symbolize connections to European royalty or aristocracy, and translate to respect. More specifically, light skin could place a slave in a favored position as the plantation master's mistress or as a house slave which could translate into more food, better clothing, or lighter workloads... During periods of increased "black pride," light skin has been seen as a symbol of mixed heritage, being a bastard, or being the product of the rape of a black woman by a lower-class white man. At various points light skin has been associated with illegitimacy and disrepute.

—Susan Marie Jenkins,
"Is Light Really Right in the Lives of Afrikan-Americans? A Review of the Psychological Literature"

What I try to do in my classroom is create an environment where kids can take risks, where they can take chances, where they are not going to feel humiliated, put-down or embarrassed. And, if they do, maybe it is only going to happen once or twice, and they'll realize from first-hand experience that the person sitting next to them is just as terrified. And that I'm just as terrified. Yet we learn, a day at a time, a little bit at a time; the fear gets chipped away and we become empowered.

—Bernice Lee, *Visionary Voices*

A Child's Daydream

Jacasta Cummings

It all started with my son Marcus's behavior at his *expensive,* new pre-school. I was working like a dog to pay for this boy's education, and he was clowning. The teachers couldn't get him to cooperate; every day they had something new to report. We had several meetings; they tried to blame his behavior on some problem at home. The child didn't have a problem at home. He had a problem at school, but they wanted to know what we were doing.

This went on for seven months, and then Marcus came home saying he wanted to be white. He even had a white-zapper, a part off of his Ghostbusters car about six to seven inches long with two plastic pieces coming from it. It kind of looked like a wand. His daddy and I had conversations with him about how God made us Black and together we made Black children not white.

I called a meeting with his teachers and told them that for some reason Marcus was uncomfortable being Black and wanted to be white, like the majority of the children in the school. There were several interracial kids, and a couple of other Black children, but with the exception of one little girl, he was the darkest child there. I told them I thought this had something to do with his behavior problem.

They listened to my concern and essentially told me that I was crazy. They even tried to make comparisons with the way children daydream. Oh, please! One teacher told me that some days her daughter wanted to be Superman and another day a doctor and another a ballerina. I asked her, "Has your child ever come home wanting to be Black?"

And she was like, "No, but it is kind of the same thing."

I said, "No, it's not the same, because your daughter can be a ballerina and all those other things—except maybe Superman. My son cannot be white."

She didn't say anything after that; I didn't have anything more to say to them because they wouldn't address the issue. If I had talked to them anymore, I'd have flipped that woman over the desk. I considered taking him out of the school but left him there because he only had a month-and-a-half to go.

Marcus didn't always have these feelings. He was just fine in his first preschool, which was mixed but mostly Black and had Black teachers. In trying to do the best thing for my child, I put him in a situation where the people, whether they meant to or not, made him feel bad about being who and what he is. They could not face it, and I couldn't ignore it. It made me feel pissed off. They refused to accept my scenario of what was going on. They just wanted to dismiss it as Marcus being incorrigible; somehow this was all his fault. They even told me that he was not ready for kindergarten.

The teachers were so insistent about his bad behavior, his lack of preparedness, and ability to function in a normal classroom setting, I went to the board of education to have him placed in a special education class. A woman there talked to him for five minutes and she asked, "Who told you he was Special Ed?" I told her the whole story. Shaking her head, she said he was very bright and that no "normal" classroom was normal anyway . She tore up the paperwork and suggested what she called a "country club" school right next door to my house for him. She said he would do just fine, because affluent children are not expected to be "normal." This white woman was like, "Oh, girl, get out of here." She thought I was the one who needed Special Ed.

After I realized what was happening to my son at school, I got him books, like *The Black Snowman*, in which a child hated being Black because he was poor. Marcus could relate to Jacob, the boy in the book, because he understood not wanting to be Black. Knowing he wasn't the only one with feelings like those made it easier for him to talk about them. But nothing changed.

He kept going on and on with his wand and wanting to be white. I was so angry, and it was so painful to see. He would zap the entire family white, one by one, on a regular basis. It was driving me crazy. I ran out of explanations. It got to the point of "This is the way it is. Get over it!" I had no more ideas about what to do.

Finally a friend who was about the same color as Marcus, a woman he liked a lot, told him that she had been through the same thing when she was a child. She explained that because of the way America treats Black people, a lot of children go through a time in their life where they want to fit in, to be white. She remembered how she felt and told him. She said that other people of color often felt the same way. She even told him about the character Whoopi Goldberg created who wore a white slip on her head pretending it was blonde hair. "Marcus," she said, "there was no happiness trying to fit in where you couldn't be yourself." After time passed, she promised him he would realize that being Black was one of the greatest things he could be. So was being Asian, Mexican, and a bunch of other nationalities. Marcus didn't understand how they could all be the greatest. She told him being yourself was the best thing anyone could ever be.

Some weeks later, we were out for a walk and my son told me, "You know Mom, being Black is not so bad." He stopped zapping us white. After that, I don't know if Marcus's behavior at school changed, but they began to tell me how cooperative he had become. The school never dealt with what it was doing to make my son not want to be Black, which made me wonder if he had ever behaved as badly as they said. Maybe intelligent, strong-willed Black children make them nervous. I don't know, I'll never know, the time has passed, but I still think about it.

Oh, I put Marcus in kindergarten against their "better judgment" where he did quite well. My son is now in second grade performing beautifully, even though he is a year younger than all of the students in his class. So much for their judgments. And he stopped zapping us white.

I don't know if this is the kind of story you are looking for, but it is the kind of story that is important to me. It is about how this world tries to mess with the minds of children, and that is a sin. It's bad enough what it has done to the grown people.

Jacasta Cummings is a twenty-seven-year-old secretary and mother of two sons.

Carletta Wilson, Spring 1986

When I Awoke the World Was Dreaming

Carletta Wilson

I identify myself. No other I but I, who is, in this instance, American born with the blood of Africa, the Caribbean, the American South, and who knows what else, coursing through my veins. This I has the audacity to consider articulating her thoughts, feelings, and interpretations about the workings of this world onto paper. And, having done so, is so brazen as to expect these thoughts to be published, read, collected, and discussed as if I had anything significant to say about the life thrust upon me from within…from without. Daring, if you will, to contemplate, to question the underpinnings of a society in which I am counted among the sleeping unbeautiful. But who, one fitful night, discovered that for years, centuries even, she lay dreaming in a land that had fallen into a deeper sleep.

I came to wakefulness slowly, kissless, in a small dark room. In glimpses and glimmerings, not quite dreaming, not yet awake I pulled up the shade, threw the latch, pressed my shoulder into muted glass, and pulled, pulled until the ancient crusty frame crumbled and grimy opaque shattered glass fell upon my feet. Bare-bodied and bleeding, I gazed upon a brilliant world. As far as I could see, in the neon's bright glare, the whole city (the world perhaps), while garishly alive, was in a stupor as drugged as sleep, as dense as dreaming.

Let me be more specific. Let's say a very attractive black-skinned wild-haired loud-mouthed colored girl is screaming at the top of her lungs at the bus stop as her friends stand, centimeters away. She screams to them nevertheless. They take no offense, but you do. Thinking, "My God! Are they always so loud…uncouth…untrained…etc.!" You turn your head in embarrassment. No child you know acts like that *ever*.

What then about a shyish girl who tries to disappear in the shadow blue of you when the rowdy crowd spies her standing next to you. They grandstand, taunt, spite, and tease. Your eyes meet for seconds and then, precise as bullets, they hit their mark.

You fear for your safety. Think how massively built the girls of today are; their movements, their danger carelessly wide.

And yet, they are silent, silenced. Their silence the silence of the unexpressed. Midst the boisterous noise of their lives this greatest silence. A worldlessness of mind. An atrophied speaking. A muteness, inarticulateness encouraged, cultivated, manufactured in how many schools and homes?

Within the overcrowded din, who attempts the act of speaking? How many voices lost within the rustle of thousands of marked and graded papers escape into corridors and corridors of huge echoing halls?

For girl-who-is-all-mouth, nothing spectacular falls from her pen, yet something in the effort makes her feel good/makes her want to try again. She tries her hand at a few raps (which she says aren't poems), poems (*real* ones), and stories. Eventually she drops her pen but manages to hold onto the *World of Poetry* anthology she borrowed months ago from the library. In fact, she's kept the book so long, not only is it overdue, but she's afraid she'll never be able to pay the fine. In this initiation of possession she is wont to say, "I kept it too long." Instead she hides the book and will not discover it again for years. Afraid to borrow another, she does not venture into a public library again for years. Instead, she reads books her mother buys from secondhand stores—dank, dusty books that release their secondhand smoke every time she turns a page.

For disappearing-girl, there is the fog that greets her upon opening her bedroom door, swimming upstream. Schools where she is just slipping by, swimming upstream, not daring to look back, or around. She's just along for the shivery ride, the coming back and forth from school in a clang of textbooks where a face like her never appears. Nor do teachers who reflect her particular beauty. Still, when she takes her pen to the page there is that electric feeling. A delicious pulse that cascades as she imagines. And as she imagines, the miraculous hand holding the pen moves.

Some children possess an ancient, invisible knowledge. Knowledge that once swept through the forests of their ancestral lands. Knowledge that seeks, now, to weave through the tendrils of these virgin lands of breath, of mind, of flesh. It sits with them in classrooms, caresses them more gently than a boy's hand on a young girl's breast. And waits. Waits within and watches. Will flower or fester, but not be denied.

How I lie. This is conjecture. Absolute invention . These are fictitious lives. I suggest you view these words as one would a prism. Fractured. Askance. Yet, this fractured view could reflect an image of any dark girl's story given the economic deprivation, the educational minimalism, lack of continued and demonstrated support for their lives. There are exceptions, I know. There are always exceptions. But hundreds, thousands, literally millions of young women of color are expected—like their mothers, sisters, cousins, grandmothers, and aunts before them—to get *through* school, marry *some* body, have *some* children, find *some* job, and to live out the rest of their lives harboring dreams in suitcases stuffed in the closet of their minds for an escape into a future never realized, never seen.

There are moments, however, in some child's life when she is peculiarly glanced at for inarticulately wanting something she cannot define, but the kernel is there. The virus is festering. Her people sense it in her keen as dogs. Within her small insular community are beacons, signs: the aunt who once strove to become a painter, the neighbor who turned the driveway into a stage and put on plays. Briefly, she sees sparks of a new life glimmer, rise, and fade.

The future of so many young artists of color goess unenvisioned because their present is so immediate, so demandingly alive. Taking huge chunks out of that man and woman so that what's left over for the girl are fractious hours on ends of long, grueling days. When she goes to bed, she goes alone save the dreams/those visions/rising from her pillow/escaping into the nighted room/howling and stuttering through the shafts of her bones until she is stunned into wakefulness by her mother's startling shaking of the bed, whipping off of the bedcovers, and exposing her near-naked body to the bright/chilled morning room.

I wish I could tell a story that's true. Of a young woman, perhaps, very dark, with African features and a name like Deborah. Or a child with a name like Claudine, whose great-grandmother is Cherokee. Who, the day she announced she was going to be a writer, joined the entire family as they cleared out the basement, set up a desk beneath its only window, purchased a typewriter, and left her alone. Alone for hours on end in that cool subterranean sphere, her visions came streaming so loudly she feared they could hear; all the way up the stairs, they could *hear*.

No one has ever told me such a tale. Women I know have had to remain private and protective of their visions until they were strong enough to bear them out up and against husbands or lover, children and others, fathers and friends, publishers and brothers. A world of people who exclaim, "But *you* can't make a living doing that!" or "Where'd you get *those* ideas?" Or they simply exclaimed, "*You* wrote this!?" And her own demons shouting, "What you twisting your little brain so for? Who you think *you* are, girl?"

I am not speaking of young Alice Walkers who walk out of the millions courageous enough to slip poems under an opening door. I speak of those young women for whom there is no door because no one imagines her as artist. She just doesn't appear to be the "type." Her family or history doesn't bear any indication of the possibility of artistic or academic success. No prince—or princess, for that matter—is expected to knock at her door. The magic belongs to another tale, told behind some other door, which she's not meant to hear because "Don't nobody want you anyway." No magician comes, witches seal their towers, fairy godmothers stay at home.

All that remains is the box—not one to be opened by our innocent Pandora, but to be turned on, by hand or remote, and gazed upon, and studied. A square crystalline ball that, in glowing technicolor, tells a never-ending story of another girl, another world.

So you are sitting in a room waiting for the reading to begin. Who is reading? How many dark faces do you see? How many Native American, Latina, Asian American? How many Euro-American? African American? Who has come to hear her read? What is she talking about, anyway? What is the substance of her language?

Who's publishing her? Are her manuscripts solicited? Is there a "market and audience" for her thoughts? Is her text "too black, not black, not black enough?" Is she perceived as "too intellectual, too shallow, too white?"

Does her work conform to the images that publishers, large and small, expect to be present in the work of a "minority" writer? Does her work fail to fall within the unwritten guidelines of her own people? If she writes about the natural world, does that make her an "uncolored" poet? Is she not allowed to stumble toward the vision? Is she not allowed to fall in the abyss to be created and recreated from the dust of our lives and somewhere within that darkness discover what truths had fallen in? Who can she satisfy if she can't find her name because the book has been lost, tossed, never written, and denied its due in her *own* mind.

Who has awakened the child, unveiled the girl, cast the woman from her parents' home? Who stays with her as she carves their names upon page after page? As she graffiti's image after image in bright, fluorescent color. As she accepts, yes, that they are; alcoholic, driven crazy, belligerently angry, educated, uneducated, well-off, poor, sane, drugged and dripped out—out of work, out of life, out of love and working. Working into life and living what's left with as much pride as they and she can muster.

More than one black girl is stunned as she awakens to the knowledge that she, her family, her friends, her children even, have accepted distorted truths, distorted histories—sold on television, on the radio, on page after page of books, in films, magazines, and newspapers which never tire of efforts to diminish us—and denied the truths of their lives.

Death is the greatest silence, is it not? The visions are not silent. They persist in unveiling the lies. We feed on them as they feed on us. Symbiotic visions germinating in the girlchild, sprouting in the young woman, branching out, blooming, fully-leaved as age carves the thick/black bark.

We are trees. Old-growth, ancient standing forests in a society that conspires, consciously and unconsciously, to erase the reality of our dreams, our lives, our histories, a society that logs and mines our lives for economic and recreational pleasure only to deny who we are.

But, I tell you. As trees standing by the water, I tell you. We shall not be moved—or logged, starved, drugged, or blipped out of existence. If there is any carving to be done, it will be our own intricate carving upon our own peculiar bodies. We shall mine our own cavernous lives. Make paper from the pulp of our flesh, pens from the stands of our bones, and ink our blood across the pages of time until computers in every classroom hum our names, and the girlchild before the screen sees herself sprouting and budding among the electric roots we've claimed. Astute in the technological air of the future, we'll redden her hands with the green of our earth. Set her mind afire with visions that galaxy into unknown dimensions. Forge desktop publishing in the palms of her hands and send her now-decrepit silence screaming through the panoramic nightmares of those asleep, yet asleep, they walk, they worry, they vandalize this world.

Carletta Wilson is currently completing, continent of desire, *her first poetry manuscript. Her poetry most recently appeared in* Uncommon Waters: Women Write about Fishing.

What we need is to teach ourselves to recognize the existence of historically specific forms of racism: to think in terms of racisms instead of an idea of racism that doesn't change through history; to think in terms of racial formations rather than eternal or essential "races." Then, perhaps, we can begin to see how an apparent commitment to diversity in a university can be engaged very intimately in a new form of racism. The important thing to remember about racism is that it promotes a transformation of the whole ideological field in which it operates, and this is what I would argue has happened in relation to changes in curriculum.

—Hazel V. Carby, from speech at Barnard College
"The Scholar and the Feminist" Conference

Bitter with a Touch of Kahlua

Four Women with a Mac

This fall, when the Ku Klux Klan was distributing pamphlets we were abruptly reminded of the thing that people of color in the U. S. must never forget; we must constantly struggle simply to exist.

In this nation of millions, non-whites have no place, and yet we persist in remaining here. Our continued presence on the periphery is a threat to white society; they have organized on local, state, and national levels, systematically destroying people of color in an effort to "purify" the nation.

When we protest, we are alarmist. When black men are brutalized by law enforcement officers, it is an isolated incident. There is a preponderance of isolated incidents in this country and because of that we must begin the struggle anew, looking for new ways to fight a very old and very stubborn battle.

—4 Bitter Women

"Only justice will stop a curse..."
—Alice Walker

January 17, 1993...
Peaches—9:00 P.M.

(I'm awful bitter these days...)

Listening to Stevie Wonder sing songs from the "Key of Our Lives," I realize that we are so rich as a people, and that, no doubt, would explain white women who are so enthralled with BLACK...Gimme that BLACK music, BLACK gear, BLACK hair, and lest I forget, the almighty BLACK DICK.

Ain't nothin' goin' on but the rent and lord knows that it's far too high...

Screwdriver—9:27 P.M.

Continuing in that vein. When will "feminism" as we know it have something to do with bitter Black girls from the city? I want feminism to be scary, maybe I'm very used to Blackness, but I want people (men) to have to deal with, come to terms with, and *try* and explain/excuse themselves to women. With Feminism, I tend to be fringe, very familiar territory, because I'm not some crunchy-ass white woman who doesn't want a door held. I'm Black as fuck; the beat that runs under "Gangsta Bitch" moves me, and I

65

don't really care to discuss sexist rap with white people.

Not only am I not with the swirl, I'm tired of whack People of Color…

Tide—10:58 P.M.

(ebb and flow, motherfucker, ebb and flow)

Dirt, dirt, dirt. That's what too many East Asians in this country have been eating. Dirt. Eat it. Lick it. Love it. Want it. And we do. Is there any one individual of East Asian descent that does not desire the white world out there? As if white could be anything desirable.

But don't talk to me about shit or dirt or any 'o' that crap. What could anyone tell me about it that I don't already know or suspect? It's no ooooordinary shit/dirt/crap, its WHITE PEOPLE'S shit, dirt, and crap. It's white, like them, ugly, like them; crusty, like them; flaky, like them; intolerable, like them; infuriating and incomprehensively disabling. Like asbestos that corrodes my lungs of iron and infects my mind, inhibits the blood coursing through my veins.

Git off, white punk. Git the fuck off me you white Nazi fascist. When you gonna learn to stop exploiting me. With your filthy hands, your frenzied mind. Don't you call me Suzie Wong. Don't think I like it when you call me your Dragon Lady, your little China Doll. I am not little, there is nothing little about me. I am a woman. I am many angry women. I am generations of Chinese daughters considered useless. Drowned at birth, sold for two bags of rice, prostituted for a handful of soybeans.

And when I say white women don't know, they don't. Don't even think of arguing with me. Because if you ask me, challenge me with the question "what is it they do not know?" then you have already lost. If they do not know, they are clueless and have no right to question my authority, my experiences, or my hatred.

My all-encompassing beauteous animosity stems from the ignorance I was taught. As if I would be so dull and lifeless as to be disinterested in the education of my very own soul. Everyone thought being considered white was a privilege. And everyone thought that if they told me they considered me white, I would be happy. Nobody noticed when I set my jaw hard, and nobody noticed as I flexed my body and shifted my weight in my chair. Did I even notice? Hell, yes.

I AM NOT WHITE. I NEVER WAZ. I NEVER WILL BE.

Keela—2:00 A.M.

Anglo bitches, we're not in Kansas anymore.

You dare to call me passive. I WILL SHOW YOU PASSIVITY. I will passively twist your insecure, displaced words and wrap them tightly about you scrawny neck. I don't need your input, nor your weak and blurry ideas on freedom for all womyn. Sometimes its not so easy getting through that thick skull of yours.

(Hold on while I get the jackhammer.)

Screwdriver, Tide—10:25 A.M.

(Jan. 23, 1992 on your calendar but really, Happy Chinese New Year!)

Well, another week has afforded new and wonderful insights about whiteness, the eternal feminine, and the world.

I am confused by you, my kind white benefactors. Do you try to lie and contradict yourselves? or can you just not help it? When England was so fucked up that some of you left, that was understood. Plainly, in any situation where white people (led by the illustrious white man) are unhappy, they should change the situation. But now you've fucked up my shit, and you don't even want me to say you fucked it up, that you're fucked up.

DOG DON'T GET MAD CAUSE YOU CALL HIM A DOG!!!

—*Daughters of the Dust,* J. Dash

I don't understand how a people so damn bent on owning everything can take other people's land. In 1948 white Europeans decided it would be a really good idea to take a Brownie country. Hence the ever problematic Israel. It's stolen goods just like me.Let the record show...I'm only gonna say it once...This is SCREWDRIVER calling YOU a DOG!!!

The tide is coming in...

The problem with white people is that they always think they're right, yet they are unimaginably ignorant. Euro-America is forever fucking us over cuz all these evangelists are incessantly super-imposing their beliefs on us as if ignoring the differences would feed a healthy understanding.

Don't look at me like I'm white cuz I'm not! When you look at me, see me. See my differences, recognize my culture. And when this process has begun, then a true relationship will be established. No Brownie can approach/address any white person without approaching/addressing Euro-imperialism and rape.

Okay, okay, white person. I said it. White. White. Now, honestly, I have nothing against white people. In fact, I know a few white people. I have white friends. I live next door to a white family, and I tell you, they have never given me any trouble. But when I drive through that neighborhood, I drive with my briefcase open, or with my gun in my lap.

But enough, I have something to say and I'm not gonna be quiet about it. (No more quiet anger, no more frustrated silence. I want loud. I will be loud. Loud in my anger, boisterous with my venom.) Put me in a room full of white people. I don't know what they are thinking; I don't know what drives them; I don't know what they are made of. But. You will see me inter-act, relate, humor, and amuse them. Now. Put a white person in a room full of Brownies and see her squirm. No white person can truly relate or even get by in a room full of Asian or Black people. Excuse me, what am I saying? No white person would ever be in a room full of Brownies. Yeah, they'd be out in the hallway.

I'm about to drive in the last screw…Yoko Ono once said that "woman is the nigger of the world," to which Alice Walker responded, that makes her a "nigger nigger." Alice, Yoko, and the whole Bitter posse are nigger niggers. Women of Color. And we'll thank you once more Mr. White Man for strip-ping us of so much. Now…we can be honest.

"WE AIN'T GOT A FUCKING THING TO LOSE!"
—The last word from the MOVE compound Philadelphia, PA, 1984

And I'll thank you Mrs. White Man for worrying about Barbie's breast and waist measurements without ever letting your pretty little white head consider the fact that if feminism is about Barbie-looking you, it still doesn't get around to me. Strange…I'm not a woman, but I can be exoticized. I'm your dad's chocolate fantasy; I'm the Asian woman your son has objecti-fied; I'm you're brother's Latin whore. I was once so foolish as to believe that women were really all the same, but if you won't acknowledge me as a woman, I can't call you anything but white.

I'm not sure we are being fair to white men. Why should they take any responsibility for their actions? There are endless possibilities for the white man. It's hard having so many options, so much control. I mean a young white man can be anything—I mean anything: a thief, an army commander, a landowner, a failure, a People of Color-fucker-wither. Look at Nixon. He was all of that at once, and he still gets mad props.

Who else could turn the world into the hell white men have created with-out being white men?—that very unusual combination of a need for control and extreme babyish. I'll give it to you. You're dangerous. But we're bitter.

Keela—10:00 P.M.

How many of you walk the face of this earth and place the constant fear and anxiety within our souls. We tell ourselves, *ye sohab khatum hojygha, dheko me sohab cheez achaa hurdoonghee.* But the fear, it is always there. It is there when you hear the front door shut and the footsteps find their way toward you. It is there when the lies to protect yourself catch up and dete-riorate the inner lining of consciousness.

Sometimes *meri Ummi* becomes the white man, catching me in the corner, asking me questions she knows I will not answer…You see, if I did answer these questions I would only be holding up a mirror in front of her face…showing her all the things she knows are there but does not want to admit. She beats the questions into me, testing me, trying to break me. She is a violent contradiction, and it accumulates within her soul. She inflicts further violence, afraid that what she has created will come back to destroy her.

Mr. White, *Angrez ke owlad*, as you punch her face and feel her blood against the palm of your hand, do you feel afraid? Do you wonder whether she will forget your face, your breath, the pupils of your eyes? Does it bother you that she will find you one day and destroy you? You may never see her face again, but it will speak to you while you sleep. You will become paranoid that she is everywhere…out to destroy. It will make you crazy, bichara, white man. She will never forget, and neither will you.

Peaches—2/3/93

How I would love to course through your veins, searing your blood (I hear it's blue), erasing your presence from my essence. How I would love to make you feel a fierce pain as you burned, from your liquid inside, to the pale of your white exterior. Sometimes I dream of your silent scream as I extract the payment that my ancestors have required, a pound of flesh for a pound of flesh…at last, your blood for my mother's blood, and her mother's. Vengeance is mine, and it will not be a god who grants it to me. I will stride forth and take what was always mine, what you ripped from my mother's womb as you whipped her for not picking cotton fast enough, as you beat her for not wanting to be isolated by your filthy hands. The dream is rich and vivid, and as the time approaches, the images are more focused, and I ache because I can taste you burning in my mouth. The sweet scent of your scorched soul lingers, and I wonder what joy is this.

are you afraid?

"Tide" is a nineteen-year-old, Chinese American student from Boston.

"Keela" is a Muslim Indian, born in India. She is a twenty-one-year-old English and computer science major with plans to attend law school after graduation.

"Peaches" is Jamaican/Nigerian, twenty-three years old, a college grad, and a classical pianist. She will be attending the Liszt Academy in Budapest.

"Screwdriver" is a nineteen-year-old African American woman of Caribbean descent majoring in English and comparative religion.

Nellie Wong

Toss Up

Nellie Wong

You call me into the hall.
Standard procedure for a conference
between a supervisor and a secretary.
You ask: If we had a fight
whose side would you be on?
His, because he is Chinese
or mine
because I am a woman?

*How can we separate our race from our sex, our sex from our race?
And we hear again and again we must struggle against sexism at the
exclusion of racism.*

*To remain private with change is to self-destruct; to go public with
change is to begin to challenge the forces of white supremacy.*

—excerpts from *Under Our Own Wings*, Nellie Wong

Nellie Wong is the author of two collections of poetry, Dreams in Harrison
Railroad Park, *(Kelsey Street Press, 1977) and* The Death of Long Steam
Lady *(West End Press, 1986). She is co-featured in the documentary film
"Mitsuye & Nellie, Asian American Poets", and she traveled to China in 1983
with the First American Women Writers Tour hosted by the Chinese Writers
Association. Her work has appeared in numerous anthologies and journals
including* This Bridge Called Called My Back, Writings by Radical Women
of Color, The Iowa Review *and* Making Waves.

The struggle of women of color for psychological and physical survival extracts a high price, and the cost goes up when the women are immigrants as well. Survival, as a woman and as a minority group member, is in itself a form of resistance. Survival for Asian women in America has taken many forms, from scrubbing floors to picking berries, from suppressing anger and swallowing loneliness to saying it is all right to look the way they do. Yet there has been much more than mere survival; there has been a whole history of resistance. Private forms of resistance pass by unnoticed precisely because myths, such as the passive Asian woman, may cloud our vision.

—Sucheta Mazumdar, *Making Waves*

Racism Doesn't Grow Up

Joyce Lee

I came to Portland, Oregon, in 1969 from Hong Kong. I came with my mother and my two brothers, and was placed in school almost immediately after I arrived. I was in a K-5 school in a working-class neighborhood, where I experienced my first inkling of cultural misunderstanding and ignorance. I remember standing next to the bathroom, in front of the children's coatrack, immobile, for an entire school year. I had no friends and didn't talk with anyone, including the teachers. After a few months, the teachers didn't talk to me either. I just coexisted in the room, me with the coatrack, the other children with the teachers. If a classmate gave me any attention, I stood as still as possible, wanting him or her to think I wasn't a real person. I'd gladly have been an inanimate object, which I emulated as best I could. Eventually the classmate would lose interest. It got to be an understanding between myself and the class. They would treat me like a statue and I would behave like one. Actually, they treated me better than a statue; I didn't get vandalized. And, because I was a statue tucked away in the corner, I was never in anyone's way. I didn't make noise and tried not to blink or move. I was actually content with the arrangement. I was even more content to stay home but ended up in that school every day for no reason I could see.

I don't remember what happened at the end of the day. I think my mother must have come by to pick me up. When I saw her, I was human again.

If I had to use the bathroom, I waited until I thought no one was looking, used it as fast as possible, and returned to my corner.

It must have been frustrating for kindergarten teachers to have me in their class. They were probably at a loss as to what to do, since I didn't respond or participate. They decided that I was mentally retarded. My mother, who spoke no English, was told that I would be enrolled in a school for retarded children. She was horrified, but she couldn't convince my teachers that I was normal. My aunt, who did speak English, couldn't convince them either.

Out of ingenuity and desperation, my mother told me to fold lots of paper boats and birds in school. She taught me every paper boat she knew, every bird, frog, pig, and so on. (I already knew how to fold boats. Paper boat races are common among little children in Hong Kong.) When I displayed my origami skills at school, I was saved from "Special Education."

What happened after this time is a little fuzzy. I remember that there was a different attitude toward me. The other kids didn't think I was dumb anymore. I still didn't talk, but eventually a special effort was made to integrate me into activities, an effort to which I responded. There was also a special effort made to teach me English, which I had not understood before. When I grasped a little bit of the language, I started to excel in class.

Looking back, I try to understand why I refused to budge from my spot. I suspect that I distrusted everyone. With the exception of one American-born Chinese girl who spoke English, no one else looked like me. I also didn't understand the language, the interactions between teacher and student. In Hong Kong, corporal punishment and mental abuse were common at school. To write the Chinese character "father" wrong meant a couple of slaps on the hand and face. If you persisted in writing the character wrong, you would lose bathroom privileges or lunch privileges. And that was in a nursery school. The Oregon kindergarten teachers, by contrast, didn't discipline the children. I didn't trust them.

Whoopi Goldberg has a standup routine in which she plays a little Black girl who wears a mop on her head because she wants to be White. As I was growing up, I wanted to be White, too. After third grade the kids became meaner and meaner. If the other kids made fun of me in second or first grade, I didn't know enough of the language to be offended or hurt. After third grade, I knew a lot of English, and the treatment seemed to get worse. "Chink," "slanty eyes," "Jap," "Hong Kong phooey" were names I grew up with. When I wasn't called those names, I was sometimes beaten up after school by one or two kids waiting for me. Surprisingly, I was beaten up not just by White kids, but also Black kids. In fact, the Black kids were worse than the White ones. The White ones would take me on singularly, but the Black kids were often in groups. When I reached high school, the racism I encountered continued—although I didn't get beaten up anymore.

By high school, White kids and Black kids segregated, they had nothing to do with each other, except in school sports. The racial hatred toward me was from the football jocks, not the jocks who were from educated middle-class families, but primarily jocks from poor blue-collar families. There were quite a few of these guys. Some of the girls on the cheerleading team, from middle-class families, also hated Chinese people.

My school had racial and economic class gaps the width of Idaho. We had a program for Asian refugees from Cambodia, Vietnam, and Laos. We also had a program for juvenile delinquents, who had a choice of attending institutions or attending my high school. On the other side of the spectrum, we had programs for young scholars who were too advanced in certain subjects to continue high school and had the option of attending Reed College for a few courses on scholarship. With this ethnic, academic, and class diversity, one might have expected a little more sophistication, more openness to differences. Unfortunately, this was not the case.

The refugees were hated and often targets of racial violence. Sometimes, I would see other Chinese students get threatened and harassed. I felt sorry for them but at the same time relieved that, for the moment, it wasn't me. I hated myself for a long time and was ashamed of being Chinese, was ashamed of being an immigrant with uneducated parents, ashamed of being poor. For thirteen years, I endured a constant barrage of racial slurs.

I remember one incident that was particularly harrowing. During one of our annual picnics in the park, the varsity football rednecks decided that the picnic was being "invaded by gooks" and started bashing heads for recreation. The Asian refugees, probably tired of being picked on day after day, fought back for a change. The fight turned into a race riot involving two hundred students. I avoided a pummeling that day by running out the park as fast as I could.

Even though I was on the school paper and art staff, and therefore had a little bit of a name, I was regarded as a "damn gook." I had hoped that, all the years I had endured these rednecks had built me some kind of immunity. I was an active student, a student who had something to contribute on *their* terms. I was a senior at that time and had distinguished myself from the refugees, primarily to show that I wasn't like them. I was really "American."

High school is horrible enough to endure, with the popularity contests and desperate conformity, but add the elements of race and class, and it is unbearable.

My high school wasn't too different from any other high school in America, nor were my experiences particularly special. I had it better than many immigrants in this country, and I am aware of that.

What I find incredible after all these years is not so much the racism I encountered, or even the violence and hatred against my people, but the institutional blind eye to that racism. Violence committed by ignorant individuals against other individuals is bad enough. Worse that that, the educators, school administration, and parents of those jocks did nothing about the racial problems at our school. Instead, the race riot in the park was hushed up. There was no open discussion of what happened, nor of the general student mentality. After the riot it was just another day at school.

Today, in San Francisco, I run into an occasional racial slur—although not to the extent I did when I was younger. The so-called "Asian invasion" is the label attached to Asians who are able to accomplish the same goals that Euro-immigrants accomplish. I've encountered a few resentful Whites. However, most of the damage from my childhood manifests itself in more internal ways.

My low self-esteem—my feelings of insignificance—are qualities acquired from childhood in America. Feelings of inadequacy creep up when I date a White guy; guilt accompanies us to a movie or restaurant. I'm paranoid that all White women secretly hate me. I feel inadequate around educated middle-class people in a social setting, so I overcompensate by putting on a confidence mask. "Oh, yes, I am educated, too, and I grew up in a mainstream family. Oh, yes, we celebrate Christmas, of course—my family lives in the suburbs." I do feel stupid when this happens because my conformity is transparent. The mask of confidence is thin.

I would be kidding myself if I didn't acknowledge my Westernization and assimilation into American culture. My family calls me "banana," yellow outside, white inside. English is now my "first language." I spend little time in Chinatown, and have few Chinese friends. This doesn't mean that I'm not proud of my heritage and that I've embraced Western values 100 percent. I'm part of that culture that has rejected mainstream options like marriage, kids, house, suburbia—options available in both in my cultures: American and Chinese.

To totally embrace Chinese values is very similiar to a total embrace of American values: marriage, kids, hard work, steady income, house in suburbia, a set of "practical" goals. The obligation that is not part of the Western model is lifelong obligation and duty to elders. No thank you.

The greatest agony for me, even after those years in Oregon, is discovering how little things have changed. It's been approximately ten years since I was enmeshed in the Portland Public School System. The other day my little eleven-year-old cousin, who arrived from China two years ago, took me aside and revealed to me the shame she was facing in school. "There are things I don't tell my parents," she said. Reluctantly, she told me how the White kids at school picked on her, said mean, racist things to her, pushed her around. Since she barely spoke English, she had a hard time making friends; she dreads school.

What consoling words did I have for her? All I could say to her was, "It's not you, it's never you, it's stupidity. Unfortunately, there're a lot of them, and only a few of you. Just remember, I'll be there if you need to talk to me anytime." I didn't have the heart to tell her what to expect in high school. I did tell her that I went through the same things she did. I felt helpless; I couldn't offer her anymore than those few scant sentences.

Joyce Lee is a twenty-eight-year-old Chinese, working in computer graphics. She paints, draws, and takes film classes.

Racism, colorism and interracial hostility and violence are too often fueled and perpetuated by a lack of communication and unwillingness to listen to others—and the single-minded pursuit of one's own goals and needs at the expense of other people's needs and welfare. In combatting these behaviors, dialogue and a willingness to listen and trust are essential.

—Victoria Manyarrows,
"Colorism in the Indian Community"

Kenya McCullough, age 18

Speaking My Peace

Kenya McCullough

I am your worst nightmare. I am the one who lingers in your mind, whose friends and family speak out. The controversy has been stirred, the news told. My name is everywhere. People point and stare at me. They shout. They curse. I square my shoulders, while my spirit is being beaten. Ah, but I must not fall. I will not survive if I do so. So, I fight on.

You are the one who is treated like a hero. You smile and speak those words. Those words that make people believe. In You. You laugh at me, saying I'm just being silly about the whole thing. You treat me like a dog, patting me on the head. A dismissal. You're finished with me. Your next victim has already been selected, God help them.

I enjoyed working with you. I thought our working relationship was special. It wasn't. You wanted more. I didn't. You couldn't accept that. I could. Oh, but you got your way with me anyway. After you finished "working late" with me, you went away. Where was your soul?

Did you honestly expect that I wouldn't say anything? That I would become docile and helpless? Or that I would not be angry? You chose the wrong one. For I am your worst nightmare, remember?

I spoke out for myself, my race, my soul. I even shocked myself when I spoke as I did. It seemed like the natural thing to do. You chuckled and said, "Oh, what a mistake you're making." Am I? Society thinks so. I am not used to people moving away from me. This is not the sixties. I am not infected with anything. Wait, wait, maybe I am. Let's see, what is that disease called..." I think it is called DEFIANCE. You would think that society would be more open-minded, but I didn't create this world. I am only living out my life in it.

You still smile your smile and speak your words, and your people believe in your world. I do not mind, though. I have spoken my *peace*. I am a whole person, unlike you. I represent all of the victims: mothers, sisters, aunts, grandmothers, students, secretaries (note: the key word, sisters, is "secret"), career women, politicians, poor, rich, handicapped, women of color, gay, everybody. I am each and every one of them.

I asked you not to touch me, and you did anyway. I know what you did; you know what you did; and society knows what you did, whether they choose to believe it or not. You see, you and I are two different people. My conscience is clear.

Kenya McCullough, who is now eighteen, wrote this piece when she was a sixteen-year-old student at Cheney College.

Amy Kashiwabara, age five

my tactile flesh

Amy Kashiwabara

He said my skin was fine Japanese rice paper
    and I told him
it is not paper
    and you can not write on it

my skin will not crumple, except with age
or burn, except with desire

my skin is not rice
and you can not eat it

nor will it slip through your chopsticks fingers
if you hold tightly

Amy Kashiwabara is twenty years old; she moved to the Bay Area after high school from New Jersey, and is currently studying political science at the University of California at Berkeley. Her work has been published in Seventeen, Literary, *and the anthology* The Verdict Is In.

Jennifer Tseng, age four

How It Is for Us

(for Meg Williams)
Jennifer Tseng

see your Black daddy
see my Chinese daddy
see our white
mamas
so mixed-up
our stirred up
sister
we feelin stirred up too
cuz look out there
at our people:
Black, Chinese, white.
my people own the grocery store
your people buy the milk
my people think you stealin
your people give me looks.

how do we ever understand
that our people
my mama's people
our people
your mama's people
our people
white people
don't trust
either of us?

Jennifer Tseng at age twenty-four

Mona Wu

Jennifer Tseng

Of all the Chinese girls in our town, I always thought Mona was the prettiest. She looks just like one of the Vietnamese movie stars. Except Mona is Chinese. And always so smart, that Mona. Though some say she's not as smart as before. One day she rode her bike down the big hill and cracked her head open when she fell. Then she was asleep for a long time. We thought she might die. But she woke up. Only she forgot a lot of things she knew before, like schoolwork kinds of things. She had to learn things about books and numbers all over again as if she were back in time, back to being a little girl instead of the teenager she was in years.

Some say if it weren't for the crack in her head, Mona never would have married that white husband of hers. Like maybe she can't think straight anymore. Not only that, but she's gone and had twins by that man, not just one child but two. Two not-quite Chinese children. Too bad for her parents. They are both so smart and make lots of money. He's a stock broker and she sells real estate, and they both belong to the Chinese Professional Association. They are good Chinese.

Mona moved to Vermont to be with her man. Vermont. Can you believe it? The atlas says that place has the highest percentage of whites in America…99 percent! "Her poor parents" is what people are saying. Well I say "poor Mona" because where will she ever find a friend who is Chinese? No Chinese, no Japanese, no Indians, no Blacks. Poor Mona. But it was her decision, so what can I say? Dr. Chou told me her husband speaks Chinese. I should at least be happy for their children, but all I can think about is why is he so interested? I hear his whole job revolves around China. I wonder if he thinks Mona is exotic. I wonder if they do it a lot.

I bet he never saw Mona with her head shaved. I did. My whole family did. When she finally woke up we went to visit her in the hospital. She didn't look too good. You could see the black gash in her head because all her hair was gone, nothing to hide the crack in her head. Me and my white mama, and my Chinese daddy, and my mixed-up stirred-up sister, we stood there in the dark hospital room and told her how lucky she was to be alive while secretly we thought how sad it was that all her long black hair was in the trash can. She didn't even keep it. I guess it wasn't the right time to remember something like that. She must have had so much to think about, trying to remember faces, all the meanings of numbers and words. She couldn't even remember who her friends were, what they looked like. So many lost things, eyebrows and nostrils and chins, floating inside her like puzzle pieces.

When we were in the parking lot my mama said to us, "She was always so beautiful, so smart. She'll get better, she'll work hard and be just as smart as she was before; it will just take a while for her hair to grow back." We believed her because my mama works at the hospital, and she knows about bodily accidents. My sister and I believed her. My father started the car and said, "Don't kid yourself. She'll never be the same."

Now it is years later, and I have seen pictures of Mona with all her long, black hair grown back into place and her two not-quite-Chinese children looking very pretty on their birthday. But when I think of Mona in Vermont, speaking Chinese to her white man and riding her bike down the lush green hills so far away from her family, I don't know who to believe. Maybe they were both right.

Jennifer Tseng says: My first published poem came out this fall. For the last two years, I have lived in the Bay Area, where I have been involved with Aunt Lute Books and radical women.

Sexual practice has been used repeatedly to enforce hierarchies of gender, race and class. The assumption that blacks are oversexed has served to justify their subordination and control by white people, who have more "civilized" values; similarly, the sexuality of "Oriental" women, depicted as somehow immoral and different, underlined the "heathen" values of the Chinese and became yet another reason for advocating the exclusion of Asians. The myth of the "erotic Oriental" and her objectification as a sexual mannequin, born of the 1870s racist environment, continues to haunt portrayals of Asians from Ah-choi to Suzie Wong to sultry Indian princesses in the movie *Far Pavilion*.

—Sucheta Mazumdar, from *Making Waves*

Wanted

Demetria Martínez

"America I've given you all and now I'm nothing."
—Allen Ginsberg

America our marriage is coming apart
I've done everything right got my degree
Now you tell me my English won't do
America I'm not good enough for you?
Better my Spanglish than your smooth talk America
No I won't sleep with you not now not ever
Ah come on America all I wanted was a little
    adobe house in Atrisco a porchswing two niños
    some democracy
Now I read in the Albuquerque Journal you left me
    for a younger woman
Bought drugs for guns guns for drugs
Destroyed Managua in order to save it
Spied on communist Maryknoll nuns in Cleveland
America your face is on wanted posters in post offices
And I'm on sleeping pills again America
Last night I dreamed the Pentagon was a great
    Ouija board spelling REPENT REPENT
In half sleep I reached for you love but got
    only a scent of amber waves of grains
I got up for a hit of caffeine the book of psalms
and whoosh! I saw the promised land
You don't need citizenship papers there it's colored
    and smells of refried beans
Remember remember who you are America
Purple mountain majesty above fruited plains
    worked by mejicanos
America call off your dogs
America give me a green card tho I don't qualify
America forgive me if I gag your memory
    at La Paloma bar on South Broadway

America I'm 27 and tired thanks to you
And thanks to you I found God on a stoop on
      Arno St.
America you claim crime's fierce in this neighborhood
I tell you it's nothing next to your crimes
The wars we fund start at the package liquor store
      and end twice a year at confession
America I don't want progress I want redemption
Cut the shit we could be lovers again don't hang up
America I'm your dark side embrace me and be saved
Pull yourself up by your bootstraps I know you can
America I'm not all bitter I'm a registered Republican
At parties when friends ask America who? I introduce
      you explain you've had a difficult upbringing
But I can't cover up for you America get that straight
Honey its not too late it's not too late
America the ball is in your court now.

Demetria Martínez of Albuquerque, New Mexico is a journalist and poet. She is the national news editor of The National Catholic Reporter. *Her first novel* Mother Tongue *published by the Bilingual Review Press, is the winner of the Western States Award for Fiction and will be released later this year. Other poems have appeared in* Turning *and* Three Times a Woman.

Tracy Clarke

On Your Mark...Get Set...Go!

Tracy Clarke

...in order to be comfortable for Your insecure ethnic pride zone, Sisters y Brothers, do I have to proclaim a manfactured blackness to the forfeit of all else that I am?

It will devide us...
—Anita Poree, *"Why..."*

Nestled between East Hampton, South Hampton, and Bridge Hampton, Sag Harbor, Long Island, is one of the oldest summer communities in which the members of the black upper and middle classes come to reaffirm their wealth and status. Facing the mainland across the Long Island Sound, a thin stretch of beach, about ten to fifteen feet from its grassy bluffs to the water's edge, running one-half to three-quarters of a mile in length. In the early 1900s, it was home to whalers, both white and black, as well as other working-class whites. During the late forties and early fifties, black middle-class civil servants, teachers, doctors, publishers, lawyers, and midsize business owners began to settle there. Because the village was set on the sound, it was considered less desirable than the oceanfront property in the Hamptons, thus the property was sold to upwardly mobile blacks. Sag Harbor quickly became a weekend haven for black displays of conspicuous consumption.

One of the most auspicious occasions of the Sag Harbor summer is the closing festivities beachside during the Labor Day weekend. Consecrated by music, food, and a series of relay races for the children, it is the essence of the traditional black family picnic.

For young girls in their early to late teens, closing day marked not only the end of summer vacation, the end of our summer loves, and a return to our predominantly white private schools, but it also underscored the middle-class work ethic that brought our families to Sag Harbor in the first place. For me, the summers held long, lonely succession of daydreaming out on the bluff, at the end of the beach, where my father built our house, occasionally shared with a school friend brought from the city for the weekend. My perfectly permed, preppily dressed Sag Harbor peers had the creeping feeling that while I held all the right credentials, somehow there was a stranger among them.

It wasn't only that our house was at the end of the beach, and all of the other kid's homes were close together in two communities set side by side,

Sag Harbor Hills and Azurest, that alienated us from one another. Nor was it that I wore my hair in a natural, or what I considered the fashionable patterning of myself after Jimi Hendrix. The traditional feelings of a tortured teen became acute during my weekend stays; at times the trips to Long Island seemed like a death sentence. I was unwelcome in both cliques formed by the young women of Sag Harbor. Not being included gave me the feeling of being wonderfully special and terribly insecure. Not belonging made me a member of a different group: teenagers in perpetual lament perhaps. Even though I was not particularly fond of any of these girls, I sought inclusion. Once I was accepted I could choose to disregard them.

Since we were all light skinned, the *finest* girls in Sag Harbor had the longest hair and the lightest eyes. The same was true of the finest guys. The black women in Sag Harbor seemed so much like white women in their looks, style of dress, and mannerisms, it heightened my feelings of inadequacy. I lacked those physical qualities that seemed to bring popularity and boyfriends. The white girls I went to school with, and all of the Sag Harbor "beauties," were such quintessential Barbie dolls—with small upturned noses, long straight hair, and thin lips—that I doubted my attractiveness, long after I was dating. I was ever fearful I was my date's second, or god forbid, third choice.

I had the fullest lips of all of the Sag Harbor women, and that was definitely not in vogue then, never mind my sporting an afro. My lips were a constant source of ridicule. The boys would taunt me, calling me liver lips, or poking out their bottom lip and curling their tongue over their top, making ape motions when they thought my back was turned. I kept my hair in an afro for many years, not to be politically correct, but believing firmly that it gave my face balance and took some of the attention away from those liver lips. I thought if I permed my hair it would only make my lips more noticeable, bringing me more ridicule and shame. (To this day, I have family members who plead with me to let my hair grow and get it permed. A trademark of the desirable, middle-class woman.)

Such self-hating negation on the part of the middle class exists to define and maintain their status through a light-skinned "aesthetic" and speaks directly to a political system that has promised acceptance to anyone who approaches the white-male dominated standards imposed by the society. Those of us who believed the dream thought we would somehow be exempt from the overt and covert forms of racism in American society, and have subsequently been subjected to, and are now products of, the casualties of black middle-class existence.

Acceptability to American whites demands more than simply looking like them. One must also internalize every form of white Western life down to speech, music, and the emphasis placed on eurocentric forms of social etiquette and appropriateness, in order to draw further distinction between "us" (acceptable blacks) and "them" (unacceptable blacks). Shunning darker-skinned blacks, even those in the middle class, and working-class blacks of any hue, is part of the black middle-class ethos.

In the late eighties, Sag Harbor did become home to one dark-skinned family who dared to intrude upon our light-skinned bliss. They were treated with the same distance and disdain whites have traditionally treated blacks moving into their neighborhoods. The family money had been made in construction—considered crude and working class, it didn't buy them entry into Sag Harbor's social elite. Not until they installed one of the few swimming pools in the community were they able to secure a tenuous place in the social fabric.

People came to swim and party at their house but snuck off to talk badly about their hosts in secluded corners. When the rumor spread that one of their sons had been arrested, everyone fled their company. I have had to struggle with the subtle racist stereotypes I was taught about other people of color, especially dark-skinned blacks. These are things so deeply ingrained, my body no longer needs translate them into conscious thoughts. It is like learning to swim. Once mastered, I no longer needed to get into the water and think—it was automatic.

My old thought patterns, depending upon the situation, included fears of dark-skinned blacks hurting me, assumptions of them being untrustworthy, and darker women being jealous of me. Despite these stereotypes, magical powers of intellect and "super black" status were attributed to dark brothers and sisters who peppered my academic and social circles.

The black teenagers of Sag Harbor never spoke of two things: our cumulative wealth or our personal searches for a strong black identity. Although I obviously did not "belong" to most of the white circles into which I was constantly thrust, my lack of a positive black identity isolated me from other black people. I was a perennial voyeur, watching my peers in Sag Harbor seemingly successfully assimilate, and watching whites enjoying the world they had fabricated.

As a result, my middle-class peers and I can be categorized in several ways. The first is the "passers" and "want-to-bes." People like this are found in every community of color. They are usually despised not only by their people but by whites, who don't mind impersonators but don't care for impostors who expect to enjoy the same benefits as white people. Then there are the Quasi Black Militants, who, after realizing black is black no matter what its hue, become aggressively critical of the white world that has rejected them, and the black middle-class that spawned them. They accept an admixture of middle-class and "ghetto" aesthetics. With an Ivy League degree on one wall and a picture of Chuck D and Malcolm on the other, they greet you with a hearty, "Yo! What's up!" They address you with "my sistah" or "my brother," but their conversation remains centered in elitist academic principles. This posturing has little to do with healthy incorporation of black values, identity, and ideals.

More evolved—not necessarily in terms of psychological health, but certainly in terms of emotional survival—is the "stick-to-your-own-kind" crowd who, knowing the hostility of wealthy whites, and working-class blacks and whites, opt to cling to the safety of their own backyard. They surround themselves with other middle-class blacks folks and only venture out of that circle when absolutely necessary.

Those who embrace a more encompassing definition of blackness— who strive to define, with deference, blackness in ways that accept all people of color and all people from the African diaspora—are the key to our survival. My journey to this particular point of view has been fraught with several passionate identity crises.

At fifteen, I was a devout hippie (not too many of us in that milieu). I was still an object of white-liberal idealized exoticism—really not much more than something to play with. At seventeen, I was a Rasta: grew dreads, read up on Jamaica, Rastafarians, and Bob Marley. Still looking at black identity through white constructs, romanticizing an aspect of a black culture not immediately my own (although my family is from Trinidad). But it was impossible to remain faithful to a religion that supports the second-class citizenship of women. During my years at college I found that once I stopped seeking "representations" of black identity, I was free to be myself.

The notion that the essence of blackness is an aesthetic gives life to the lie that it can somehow be reproduced, put on, or packaged by hands other than black ones. As long as I bought the concept of "black" as a monolithic principle, I was cheating myself, limiting myself to a handful of "acceptable" modes of expression, all of them one-dimensional. We no longer need to accept limited definitions of ourselves, or seek to fit or force one another to fit prefabricated molds.

I once worked with a black women's poetry group at New York City's Hunter College in which the women were all black, and predominantly lesbian. Constant criticism was bandied about the women who were not lesbians in the group, or the women who straightened their hair. I'm certain their behavior would have greatly saddened the poet for whom the group was named. A woman who spent her life trying to open new dialogues amongst all women of color.

In 1989, I worked for a summer with a black theater group in Harlem.

I was eager to be there to further their goals, but their mistrust of my intentions—their belief that I, a black woman of the middle class, meant to come in and take over a black working-class organization—outweighed anything I could say or do on my own behalf. In only two weeks their attitude passed from cool to hostile. "What do you want up here anyway?" I was asked. "Don't you have something to do downtown?" It was apparent that, like my stereotyping of working-class and dark-skinned blacks, they had a list ready for the "known" behaviors of high-yella folks like me. Another woman, fresh from an all-girl Ivy League school and equally "bourgeoisie," joined the theater around the time I did, but her intentions were not questioned. Her skin was brown, and despite their affluence, her parents had not left Harlem, as mine had.

The most disturbing aspect of my stay at the theater was the group's desire to discuss or hold workshops on everything in the world (including how they could get along better with white folks) except issues of classism and colorism among us.

Ultimately, being light-skinned and middle class has denied me access to circles of people of color who are not middle class. Acceptance by blacks other than middle-class blacks was contingent upon another form of self-negation, the need to be "blacker than thou"—different from white assimilation, but still a form of posturing.

The idolization of light skin seemed to reach a fevered pitch during the mid-eighties. Weaves got longer, and blue eye contacts seemed to spring out of a Farrakhan-induced nightmare. For most, it reached its pinnacle when a black women's magazine celebrated black womanhood by airbrushing the cover girls to a coffee-cream hue. Deep-chocolate–skinned top model, Karen Alexander, appeared on the cover of a popular white magazine in all of her natural beauty and the following month showed up quite a different shade on the cover of the black magazine, notorious until the nineties for gracing their pages with only light-skinned women.

At the end of the eighties, there was a return to dreadlocks, Afrocentric instead of Eurocentric clothing, Afrocentric poetry readings and rappings—the likes of which had not been seen since the sixties.

It seems the black middle class is awakening to the fact that even though we possess all the trappings white Western culture instructs us to acquire, we continue to be denied equal rights as "Americans" because we lack the ultimate ticket—white skin. Being light-skinned and middle class was thought to give us authority over other blacks; in reality, being light-skinned middle class gains us access into only one world—the black middle class.

One of my earliest realizations that money or education were not the "great qualifier" came when I was thirteen. My parents were divorced by then. One weekend my father picked me up after leaving his office; he was still in a business suit. He planned to take me to see a movie and then out for dinner.

The theater was located under the Plaza Hotel on Fifth Avenue; we had to go down a few stairs in order to enter. As we descended, a white man hurried past us, opened the door, then promptly shut it behind him. My father straightened as I passively watched; putting his hand on my shoulder, he maneuvered me in front of him as he opened the door. As we passed the white man, who I now recognized as an usher, looked level-eyed at my father and said, "Niggers." The way he said it, flat and without direct malice, as if it were my name, raised my head; as my eyes met his, he smiled. A long, slow smile of satisfaction. Dumbfounded, I looked back at my father, who wouldn't look at me. He bought the tickets and led me into the darkened theater, found seats, and promptly returned to the lobby to "have a word" with the usher. Until this day I do not remember what movie we saw. As we left the theater, I remember the racist usher was gone. My father stepped toward the curb to get a cab. Although we were the only people hailing a taxi, and though we were standing on the eastbound side of the street, cabs repeatedly whizzed past us.

Eventually one stopped in front of us to let a passenger out. As my father tried to enter the cab, the driver turned on his out-of-service light, reached over his seat, slammed the back door, and locked it. My father attempted to shout something as the cab accelerated from the curb. The driver casually turned, gave us the finger, and sped off. Standing in front of the Plaza Hotel, I became clear about the country in which I lived and the status afforded to people of color in it. Two white men had just attempted to strip my father of his manhood, and me of my belief in equality. Although only an usher and a taxi driver, if class was the issue in America, they possessed the quality the country really most values, and it gave license that justified their behavior—white skin.

As long as we continue to rely on a white system of power, not only economically but ethnoculturally, we will be chained to internalized racism, the belief that white is right.

Three summers ago I returned to Sag Harbor for the Labor Day weekend, after not going there for almost five years. Although it was never spoken aloud, we were all aware that our fathers may be brown-skinned or darker, but our mothers were most often coco-colored or lighter—in order to give birth to the genteel, genetic dream of, if not passing, passing more easily in the white world. The perversity of such behavior is known, but the great cultural definer—skin color—is still viewed as a trump card in the game of race. The system of marrying to lighten the race, and the subtle inducements for the children of these marriages to do the same, without crossing the thin, pathological line into interracial marriage, is central to the notion of being black and middle class. Colorism and its incestuous partner, classism, has not only shaped who I am but propels me to constantly struggle with how I view the world in which I live. All these thoughts plagued me as I made my way to the beach.

The shortest way to the end of summer festivities is still through my backyard, down the stairs, and then about thirty-five yards along the cool dark sand to Sag Harbor Hills. As I walked along watching the sunset, I thought of all the things I had not wanted to think about. The way in which we try to push away our painful childhood memories, but carry them with us anyway, are reflected in our actions and how we relate to other people. Still, the idea of facing my childhood "ghosts" now grown up and leading adult lives, made me want to walk straight out into the ocean, or go back home and crawl under the covers.

The music rose up over the thick brush that divides the beach from the dirt road where the relay races are held. I could hear the laughter of small children and the murmur of lots of people speaking at the same time. I drew myself up as tall as I could and walked into the midst of the ongoing fete.

"Hey girl," I said, walking toward the group in which my cousin was standing at the edge of the dirt road. Three of the women looked at me with disdain, then at one another. My cousin smiled warmly. If she hadn't, the ocean was still a few bounds and a leap away. "What's up?" she replied, as I plopped a metal folding chair next to where she was standing. We exchanged some small talk, then turned our attention to the relay races at hand.

First the boys ages eight to twelve lined up at the end of the dirt road, preparing to race one another to the other end soon after a winner is proclaimed. Then the girls eight to twelve lined up.

I stood and moved in close to my cousin's left side. The girls, now standing shoulder to shoulder, were young, thin, and all extremely light-skinned. Some with only a hint of color.

I looked at the group of women I was standing with. We are all almond beige, not one darker then a coffee-cream. We are the previous generation. "The kids look white," I said. On your mark... Get set... Go! We both examined a girl who was running our way, her brownish-blond pigtails bobbing in the wind. "I noticed that too," said my cousin. We don't look at or say anything else to one another for a very long time.

Tracy Clarke is a writer originally from New York, now based in San Francisco. She is currently working on her first novel.

Pamela Norton and her daughter

Her Favorite Color

Pamela Norton

Her favorite color is blue. "Like my eyes, Mom," she says.

"But your eyes aren't blue anymore, Susanna."

"Yes, they are!" she flashes back at me.

I look at those blue-green, grey-yellow, hazel eyes. I think to myself, "I like *brown*." I always thought very romantically that I would have a brown child with brown eyes, dark, like chocolate, or red-brown like a leaf, and dark, dark espresso brown hair, probably in curls, with dark eyebrows and dark eyelashes and a smooth, silky brown skin somewhere between nutmeg and café latte.

I dreamed of that brown baby probably out of hearing my mother speak so lovingly of brown herself. She always wanted her skin to be mahogany. I loved to hear that word: mahogany. It had an organ-pipe sound to it: ma-ho-ga-ny. I imagined my mom getting her tan in the Acapulco sun and then rubbing it down with lemon-scented furniture oil, watching it shine black-brown with undertones of red and yellow, like a fire under the wood.

When I was ten, my mom and I really did go to Acapulco, and we both got sunburned and peeled. She was so eager to go straight to the beach when we arrived. We were so tired from the trip, we fell asleep and lay in the sun for three hours, burning away. We couldn't lie on our backs for three days.

The clean sheets, smelling of water and fresh air, seemed like sandpaper on our skin. We slept on our stomachs, matching our position on the beach days before in a quiet, dark room, the shutters closed but light coming in from the balcony. We could hear the wind on the street, feel it rushing in from the balcony, hear the boys in brown shorts and shirts playing down below, hear the cars and trucks going down the main beach street and the surf just beyond and the rustling of the coconut palms. There was a price to be paid to look so brown. We are light-skinned blacks and we look and look for brown.

I've always looked for the brown. My first husband was beautiful to me because he was brown. Long, glossy, black-brown hair with a slight wave in it, café au lait skin, deep chocolate brown eyes—everything about him seemed so fine and whole. We were told we looked like brother and sister. He never seemed to mind. It had a kind of truth to it, and I loved it. Brown on brown.

My daughter is closer to me in color than to her white-skinned dad. She is tawny, a tan kind of brown, while my arms at least are very close to mahogany. Her eyes are grey-blue. Her hair is brown, red, and white blond just around her face. She doesn't match the picture I had—and still have—of a baby of mine. Sometimes I look at her from this picture-holding place and say to myself, "Who *are* you? Are you my child?" It's an odd feeling, her being so different from me. But because of that she is very lucky. She will not blend into me as I blended into my own mother. She is her own person.

Pamela Norton is a short-story writer and poet who has been a vocalist in a poet/rock band, an ESL teacher and translator/interpreter. She currently works as a speech and language therapist. Her cultural heritages are African (Madagascan & Cameroon), Native American (Choctaw, Cree, and Creek), Irish, French and possibly Sephardic Jew on her mother's side, and Anglo-American on her father's side. This piece is about beginning a journey back to her mother's mother's mother.

We stand between worlds, those who went before, our ancestors, and those who will come after. What we do is of great consequence.

—Luisah Teish, from the film *Goddess Remembered*

Jennifer A. Hinton, 1987

Twenty Questions

Jennifer A. Hinton

Why are there still paper bag parties?

Why do people say "She was dark, but she was still cute"?

Why would a crowded busful of Black people explode into cursing and kicking and punching and pulling at a light-skinned, grey-eyed Black woman who accidentally nudged a five-year-old, dark-skinned, handicapped Black boy for whom no one was willing to yield their seat anyway?

Why would a pregnant Black woman remark, "Lord, let it be a boy because I cannot deal with no ugly, nappy hair"?

Why do Black parents on public transportation make their toddlers scramble into seats the best way they can; but biracial toddlers are held?

What would make a Black student in a white university classroom stand up and proclaim his "Cherokee/Irish/Mexican/Portuguese" blood, but not his African blood?

What happened to all the dark-skinned models with afros?

At clubs, why do Black men collect women's phone numbers and, the next day, only call the light-skinned or biracial ones?

Why do Black people say, "With his/her ugly, black ass"?

Why do Black people still say "good hair" and "bad hair"?

Why are we trying to call ourselves "African American" rather than "Black?"

When a light-skinned or biracial woman walks into a room, why do people stare and stare and stare and stare like they're observing some amoeba in a petri dish or something?

How can a Black composer of a musical opus about Malcom X be married to a white woman?

Why would someone plop a Malcom X hat over a processed hairdo or a flowing hair weave?

How can a chairman of a Black Studies department at a prestigious Ivy League university be married to a white woman?

How did Clare and Heathcliff began Sondra and Denise?

Why do Black men take their girlfriends to fancy restaurants and when a light-skinned or biracial woman walks in, they obsess about how "snotty" and "stuck up" she probably is; and when the girlfriend goes to the restroom and returns, she catches him trying to get the woman's phone number?

Why are Black people so hostile to one another?

Why after all the enlightenment that the larger Eurocentric society upholds whiteness as the definition of ultimate beauty; why after commissioned sociological/psychological study after study, paper after paper, talk show after talk show, research and more research with children with white and black dolls that conclude that colorism destroys lives, destroys self-esteem, destroys communities; why after "Black is beautiful" and Malcom X and Black Power and fists in the air and Angela Davis and "I'm Black and I'm Proud" and "I Am Somebody" and "Be True to the Gang" and that colorism is part of the plan to divide and conquer; why after this are we still consciously saying "darkie," "Casper, the Friendly Ghost," "I can't marry you; I want light kids," "Black and ugly," "Zebras," "Black women are so hard to get along with," "half-breed," "my grandmother's mother was Portuguese," "I don't allow yellows in my car," like we don't know better, like we haven't been told and taught better over and over, again and again?

Is it that deep inside we've been taught to hate ourselves so much we just can't help it?

Jennifer A. Hinton *is a graduate of Northwestern University, resides in Chicago, and is employed in a corporate library. She has authored many short stories and is currently working on a comic novel about unemployment.*

My first priority is to be true to my Self. Really searching for what I truly want. My therapist told me the Buddhist definition of laziness. Workaholism. So now I feel really inspired because by that definition most of this society is lazy. Exterior work, jobs and such take precedent over working on the Self.

— Conversation with Noemi Sohn, 1993

Sabrena Taylor, 1987

Hair 2

(for Teresa Kay Williams)
Sabrena Taylor

Our mothers tried their best to change our image
To press our hair
To relax our hair

           as if hair was
nervous
      hair would shout
          t o o
             L O U D

My mother's tongue I tried to cut with the knife of the tongue of
children who didn't understand my fair skin, my dark skin
Father's tongue
Moon eyes
My hair cried
The one little curl society could not press and repress
My image refused to be oppressed
That one little curl stood out, shouted
          t o o
             L O U D
Made waves and for that one little curl I give my deepest
appreciation
For I am alive today as I will be alive tomorrow
Making Waves

Sabrena Taylor is a poet and artist of African American and native Japanese ancestry. She was born and raised in Galesburg, Illinois, with seven siblings. Her work will appear in an anthology entitled Watch Out! We Are Talking, *by Glide World Press in San Francisco.*

Joyce E. Young's eleventh birthday

Arrogance

Joyce E. Young

Why haven't we been taught such arrogance
Or developed a sureness of self
That makes it a reflex
To look at other people's noses
And judge them to be big
Because they don't look like
Our nose, our mother's nose, our father's nose

A sureness that allows us to
Not think twice or at all
Before stating clearly and irrevocably
That another person's skin looks like mud

A sureness bequeathed to us
Along with confidence
That's everyone's hair
Should be brown, blond, or red and
Fall limply like a small wet animal
On our heads after we've taken a shower

A sureness of the rightness of self
That propels us to ask the owner
Of the big nose, muddy skin, non-limply hanging hair
To do something about his/her aberration
Like have plastic surgery, use Esoterica
And explain to us why they have to do these things

*Joyce E. Young is an African American poet, writer, and book reviewer. She
frequently gives poetry readings.*

Patricia Wong Hall, at age three, 1953

The Asian American Women's Blues

Patricia Wong Hall

Some blonde woman
    from "Dynasty" is
        on T.V.
telling me
    I, too, can be a
        blonde.
            "You're not talking
            to me...," I say.

All across America—
    yellow women,
        black women, and
            brown women
look at her
    and marvel.

Some women laugh—
    others want to
        scream.
Some throw things at their
    television sets—
others write
    their networks.

The mind-set that
    sponsored this
        commercial has also
brought us
    Charlie Chan,
        Rochester,
            Tonto, and
                Suzie Wong.

"Miss Saigon"
impels us to
end racist media now—
Protest marches
cry out
against oppression, injustice.

The fat media millionaire
gazes out his
mansion terrace.
But a riot has
erupted in the
streets below.
Justice to
the people.
The fat, pink man
gets a pink slip
Time for some new blood.

Patricia Wong Hall is a writer, lecturer, and graduate student in Arizona. Her works have appeared in Asian Week Journal, No Need to Kill *(Buddhist Peace Fellowship),* Brushstrokes, *and others. She has lectured widely on Asian American Issues, primarily in Oregon and Arizona. She is currently working on an anthology on anti–Asian American violence.*

In the old way practiced by many tribes, a person who is so inclined and capable on occasion sits and tell stories. The stories are woven of elements that illuminate the ritual tradition of the storyteller's people...The strength and sturdiness of that tradition reflect the strength and sturdiness of a people...Contrary to popular and much scholarly opinion in Western intellectual circles, aesthetics are not extraneous to politics.

—Paula Gunn Allen, *Spider Woman's Granddaughters*

Victoria Lena Manyarrows, 1992

See No Indian, Hear No Indian

Victoria Lena Manyarrows

it wasn't so long ago, i tell you in a stream
of broken words & suppressed anger,
when these lands were not occupied
they were free
and people lived in harmony

you tell me you don't
want to hear it, you don't
want to hear what i have to say

i tell you, *what you are doing to me now is*
killing me
negating my existence
denying me my voice, my life.

i tell you how we the indians always listened
listened to one another and
talked out our differences.
i tell you this world
this world strangled & distorted by white men
will die a harsh and bitter early death
if no one learns to listen
and dream together.

but you don't want to hear this
you say it's too much for you now
you've already left
your mind a stone
and the doors have closed.

Victoria Lena Manyarrows is Native/mestiza (Eastern Cherokee), born in Iowa in 1956 and raised alongside reservations and within mixed communities in North Dakota and Nebraska. Since 1981, she has worked extensively with community arts and alcohol/substance abuse programs in the Bay Area and has a Masters degree in Social Work. As a writer, activist, and artist her goal is to use written and visual images to convey and promote a positive, indigenous Native-based worldview.

The Black Latin and the Mexican Indian

Avotcja

When I grew up on New York streets
And fought my way thru knee-deep garbage
My Mama sewed stars on Amerikkkan flags
At the Brooklyn Navy Yard
Like all the other Mamas
And I was lonely

When you grew up in California fields
And listened to the fat greasy patrones
Call your Papa a "wetback greaser" —
Your Mama worked in the packing houses
Worked for pennies…so that—white ladies-
could
      wear silk stockings
Paid for with your daily hunger
Were you lonely too?

While you grew callouses on your hands
I grew a callous on my heart
And, somewhere, we lost what little laughter we'd
known
And the loneliness grew

While you picked tomatoes
I picked pockets
And we both learned how to lie & steal & fight
Some call it survival
I call it Loneliness

But one day the smog lifted
The city & the country smiled at each other
And so did we
The Mariachi met the Mambo
And so did we
And like the frozen snow in spring
We melted
And like the warm winds of summer
We were gentle
And no matter how the rain falls
And if time stops dead in its tracks tomorrow
I will praise the Gods for your existence
I will dance to your rhythms
Even as the sun grows cold
And I'm not lonely any more.

Avotcja is a black Puerto Rican born in Brooklyn and raised in Harlem. She is a poet, photographer, teacher, and musician who makes percussion instruments and plays guitar, flute and bass clarinet. She is seeking a publisher for her collection of short stories, poems and photographs entitled Pura Candela— Pure Fire.

Kimberly G. Hébert, 1992

But Who Will Lead the Revolution

Kimberly G. Hébert

"…my form is a filthy type of yours,
more horrid even from the very resemblance."
—Mary Shelly's *Frankenstein*

They took away my color…
        Beautifully brown and black
Now—pale and sallow, sickly almost,
        reduced to hiding from a sun my ancestors worshipped.

They took away my hair…
        Beautifully knotted and curled tightly to my head
Now—stringy and limp, getting in the way
        Always in my eyes, preventing my sight.

I am the pale monster, rejected and cursed,
        Forced to walk the earth, head bowed in shame,
The rape of centuries written on my face.
        I wear the mark.

How will they know me when they come for me?
I look like no child of theirs…
Unnatural, inhuman, an experiment necessitated by the will to leave
A trace
Rather that not be…

A scapegoat
Burdened by the daughters, mothers, sisters on the altar of the
pale gods—
To buy more time—
For the revolution…

The first one like me that was kept,
Why did they let it live?
Why to finally accept the formal humiliation,
Why to finally surrender
To pain?

For the price of that life, they sold their birthright…
For home will always be here…*But They can't go there…*

       Because they kept the first one like me…
Decided to take it inside,
Carry it in their womb,
Raise it and claim it as their own—
We are home—*but we can't go there…*
We wear the mark.

How will they know us
When they come to take us home?

Kimberly G. Hébert is a Ph.D. candidate in American Literature, specifically that of nineteenth-century African American women writers, at Tufts University in Medford, Massachusetts. A twenty-eight-year-old graduate of Columbia University, she is an African American who calls Baton Rouge, Louisiana, home.

It is…[a] false notion that there is only a limited and particular amount of freedom that must be divided up between us, with the largest and juiciest pieces of liberty going as spoils to the victor or the stronger.

—Audre Lorde, "Scratching the Surface"

Yet You Worship Me

Saundra Sharp

You fear my power
yet you worship me
you castrate my men
       yet you worship me
you suffer my wisdom
you refuse to honor Krishna while
you remake me with missionaries
       yet you worship me

you make suntans a status symbol
       you imitate me
you fantasize tall, dark & handsome
       you make love with me
you dip your hip in my dance
you are baptized in my music
you study my rhythm and when convenient
       you pass for me

you pay to avoid my neighborhood
       yet you worship me
you are threatened by my offspring
       yet you worship me
you negate my history
you pollute my life force and
you plant genocide on my doorstep
       yet you worship me

You are all in my blackness
and my blackness is all in you
the Pope kisses my feet
       I am the Black Madonna
I dance in my own temple
       I am the Black Tie Ball
I am larger than life

I am the Black Sea
I am incomprehensible
I am the Black Forest
I ride the fierce wind of rebellion
I am the Black Stallion

You are all in my blackness
and my blackness is all in you
I am the wine you prize
I am "the darker the berry"
I gamble with your sincerity
I am the Black Jack dealer
I am 9/10ths of your seed
I am the Black child
I am the first world out of place
I am your third eye
I am your classiest color
I am basic Black

And you worship me.

So what *is* the problem?

Saundra Sharp is a Los Angeles-based writer, poet, and filmmaker.

Dahpne Muse

The Bob—*Not an Afro, But Still a Liberating Do*

Daphne Muse

While the biweekly trip to Shirley's Beauty Shop was always an adventure, it was also a foray into a world I often entered reluctantly. Shirley was the consummate 1950s beautician. Man and money troubles seemed to plague her very existence. She also had more than her share of inconsiderate customers and complained incessantly about my long, thick "kanky" hair; the kind that seemed to resist every effort to cooperate and stand at pressed attention.

It was my mother's insistence on having the kanks tamed in my heavy, rope coarse, long black hair that put me in this world of fast tongued women with pit-viper tempers. Tranquility and calm were not characteristics associated with black beauty shops of the fifties and sixties. Gossip was thick, genuine complements rare, and social ascension a common quest.

But Shirley always greeted me with a warm smile, often followed by a finger pointing pressing comb in the hand admonishment. "Child, don't let no man turn your freshly done head and set you sweatin' it back into kanks and knots." I really didn't have a clue what she was talking about. In fact, many of the conversations, especially those about men, simply went over my head. When I was thirteen, boys were funky socks and hanging out buddies, not hormone igniters prone to make my heart hum or my "twilly go silly." The boy barriers seemed nonexistent, and I moved through their world with an athletic and social ease that often made me question why I was a girl.

The men in my world were my father, four brothers, uncles, and numerous cousins. There were also my brother's friends and the fellows who were my softball and tennis teammates. The sexual pulse had yet to develop a lifeline, and I felt an unusual equality with my brothers and male friends. I could pitch a fast knuckleball and had an awesome backhand, and simply held my own in their world.

Within two blocks of Shirley's shop, I could smell the burnt hair combined with the residue of fried fish, barbecued ribs, and hot links. Hot Lily Ann suits, Christian Dior dresses, and Schiaparelli hats regularly appeared on the arms of fast talking do rag wearin' men. On occasion, a slick suit sportin' Willie would drop by with a newly boosted fur cape or diamond ring. While there was much talk of do wrong men, there was also plenty of finger waving, chicken neckin' hand on hip posturing hot comb waving talk about not being a "don't take no mess woman."

"Honey, I told Norman the other night that if he didn't stop seeing

Charlene, there wasn't gonna be no mo' Charlene to see," said a woman with a gold star in her front tooth. Whoever Norman was, I thought he must have been crazy 'cause you really didn't even think about messin' around on no woman with a gold star in her front tooth.

Others would join the chorus with their "womanly wisdom." Sometimes, even the woman who was messin' with the man of the woman talking about the woman messing with her man would chime in with a "I know 'xactly what you mean."

Shirley's was also one of the early feminist havens where women could talk freely of their wants and their woes and not have to listen to no mess from some fist-in-your-face- testosterone-flexing man.

"I tell you honey, he can bring fur coats from now 'til 'Juvember.' But that ain't gonna make me get up off my sweet stuff no faster than I want to," was the constant refrain of one of Shirley's weekly customers, Christine Wilson. Those tacky diamonds on six of her ten fingers made me suspect of almost anything she said.

While her demeanor was often haughty and pretentious, her tongue wagged wickedly with expletives that would make a street savvy dude reel in amazement. She also claimed intimate affiliation with Washington's upper "culud" echelon and spoke of residing at the "I have a maid and eat caviar" standard of living. But she cut out the talk of caviar one day when Thelma Thompson, a plucky little woman who worked at the post office said, "Caviar ain't nothin' but fish shit."

"They's fish eggs, Thelma, fish eggs," corrected Shirley waving her hot comb in her circle of confirmation. "Yeah, and if she got a maid, I'm the Queenie of England," said Shirley, whispering into her customer's ear and waving her curling iron like a magic wand.

On this particular biweekly trip, I had arrived at Shirley's shop with a conscious decision firmly fixed in my head: Get a Bob—a hairstyle, not a man. The decision was an act of intraracial self-preservation and had nothing to do with aesthetics.

I knew "the Bob" would liberate me from the endlessly oppressive hours in the gossip riddled boosters' haven. It would also free me from Shirley's constant high sighing complaints about pressing through this tangled maze of kinks, knots, and waves.

But most importantly, it was an act designed to keep Barbara Johnson and her partners from whuppin' my high yella butt. High yella culud girls with long hair were often moving targets for their darker-hued sisters. When girls went after whuppin' your butt, hair was the first thing they went after. The second thing they went for was hair—too. I figured the less I had, the better were the chances of defending myself.

Barbara Johnson had a face full of freckles, a medium brownish henna complexion and hair that screamed the color red. She also walked with a decided bone poppin' swagger, wore "Nineteens" from Rich's Shoe Store, and without saying it in a word, let it be known that she wasn't scared of nothing or nobody. But she also had magical rainforest green eyes that remained hidden behind her sling back wearing bully stance. And she was street as well as book smart.

Her partners consisted of five girls who wouldn't breathe unless Barbara gave the command. They was bad mommas, too. But Barbara, unlike boisterous Bernice Taylor, was quietly tough and commanded a lot of attention. While she was both brilliant and witty, she had my attention but not my respect. Her unfair judgment of me saddened me and her unwillingness to know who I was, beyond my high yella skin, was also troubling.

As a fair-complexioned girl with long hair, I was socially positioned as an enemy to my darker-skinned female peers. I was often taunted because my hershey bar and black velvet skin classmates thought I thought I was better and smarter than them. The fact that I was on the honor roll only compounded their disdain and sent the needle on their "I can't stand that yellow bitch" meter up another ten notches. While I hung tough with the toughest of the boys, girls, except my cousin Sadie, struck pure fear in my soul. Drawn to sports, wearing pants, and having no interest in testing our hormones, neither of us did the girl thing well.

What Barbara and her mighty gang of five cohorts failed to realize was that my parents had taught me and my brothers that being fairer of skin did not entitle us to any more or any less than anybody else. Disparaging remarks and jokes regarding skin color were not acceptable in our home. But in 8th grade my social awkwardness, combined with my general discomfort around girls, created a barrier that compounded the perception.

On the other hand, four foot eight mint chocolate colored Pat Jones, had megathick hair that cascaded down her back all the way to her calves. She was adored, an honor student, and no one seemed to mess with her. While her chocolate skin and cable thick dark brown "had to be Pressed" hair was a bridge to building friendships, my yellow hue was a barrier to social acceptance from my bronze and beyond sisters.

Although my friendships reflected no intraracial color bias, the yellow caste of my skin and my long hair made me a moving target for the hostilities bred by insecure color conscious adults, who had inherited this internalized oppression and passed it on—generation after generation.

"Now Daphne, are you sure your mom said it was fine for me to cut this stuff?" said Shirley as she peeked around from the back of my head into my face. My tongue swollen with a lie the size of the icy December Potomac River, I looked shyly over my shoulder and said "Yes, ma'am. She said it would cost less to have my hair done if I got it cut." Shirley's posted prices were based on the length of the hair. While they often admired it, most beauticians, who had to press and curl it, had a tremendous dislike for long, thick hair.

As the lie rolled off my tongue I was certain Shirley would see it swelling inside what had become my dry cavern of a mouth. Unlike my mother, Shirley couldn't see the lie forming in my brain before it even got to my mouth.

I thought it was my logic that had worked. But she was so busy catching the last line of the latest gossip circulating around the pungent smell of residual barbecue sauce on paper plates that I probably could have told her to dye it green and she would have.

As she picked up the shears to begin the cut, a woman hollered from across the room, "You gonna cut all that child's pretty hair off her head? That gal got good hair." The notion of good hair and bad hair impaired the confidence and had critically wounded many a young short-haired black girl. It sat my teeth on edge. If it was on your head and you growed it your ownself, then it was good hair. No, that wasn't one of those things my grandmother used to say. It was just something I knew should have been so.

"If I was her momma I wouldn't let you go putting them scissors in my child's hair," yelled out a schoolteacher, licking the barbecue sauce off her fingers as she waited for her perm to set. I tried to figure out how I could take one of Shirley's irons and curl that woman's tongue back into her throat. As Shirley bent down and looked in my face, she said, "Did you bring a picture?" I handed her the pictures I had cut out of a black detective magazine and one out of *Seventeen*.

"Oh child, this thing here is too grown for you. I can't send you outa here lookin' like no ho," said Shirley, pointing to the picture in the detective rag. Shirley liked the Bob on the freshly scrubbed face of the rosy-cheeked, brunette girl in *Seventeen*. "This one is more like you. What you think?" as she started to clip at the sea of hair flowing down my back. My answer to the question mattered not.

For what seemed like an adolescent eternity, Shirley snipped, sheared, and shaped. No tears fell as thick sections of my hair fell to the floor like newly shorn wool; only signs of relief that maybe I wouldn't have to worry about getting my butt kicked because I was high yellow, socially slow, and the owner of thick braids that often got tangled in the double-dutch rope. Believe me, if Shirley could have given me a dye job on my skin, I would have taken that too; anything to temper the wrath of Barbara Johnson and her partners.

But Washington, D.C., was a notoriously corrupt city not only politically but also around the question of color. Paper bag parties were common, and if you were browner than the paper bag, you couldn't come into the party. Intraracial apartheid was common and for years remained the basis for deciding who was worth forming a friendship with and who was not.

Fortunately my parents had grounded me in some decency around many things, including the question of "the color line." While it sickened me that people made a big deal out of fair-skinned girls and women, it horrified me that I had to struggle with forming my own friendships based on intraracial victimization around color.

What I had totally overlooked was my parent's reaction to what I had done. As the last lock fell to the floor, an "uh oh" got caught in the middle of my throat. A momentary "can I tape this stuff back on my head?" flashed through my mind. The moment of reckoning was surely to be a difficult one.

Once my hair was cut, shampooed, and pressed, Shirley styled it. "Ooh, if I must say so myself, I'm a bad hair stylin' mamma jamma," said Shirley, passing the mirror around to me. My guilt about being high yellow, and my mother's admonitions about vanity, made me hesitate in taking the mirror.

The sauce laden gossip ceased momentarily as everyone looked up to see what Shirley had done to my hair. I reluctantly took the mirror in my trembling hands and looked. It was sharp. That Bob was finished off with a smooth, clearly defining line at the nape of my skinny neck.

"Honey, when you came in here you was a girl scout uniform–wearing little girl, but Shirley done cut you into a woman," came out of the mouth of Wanda Jenkins—a worldly woman who was always in the beauty shop. I guess her worldliness required frequent hair maintenance.

Despite my parental trepidation, the Bob brought me a new sense of confidence in dealing with my peers. Now, I knew that they would be able to see beyond the yellow of my skin and into the spirit of my soul to the color line lessons my parents had taught me so well. The hair that had been the blinding barrier was no longer there.

I was delighted to pay Shirley my momma's hard-earned money and bid adieu to the gossip, gaggle, and reeking smell of rancid barbecue. As I stepped on the D.C. transit bus from home, I carried that newly discovered sense of myself. What a difference a Bob made.

But as I sat down, thoughts of what my parents would say returned to my head. My mother would surely discover I had lied to Shirley. Would Shirley get in trouble? Would my mother stop letting me go to her shop? Those trips actually had some elements of fun to them because I could daydream out windows beyond my adolescent and racial confusion into the imaginary, free-spirited worlds I loved creating.

"Rhode Island Avenue," said Mr. Smooth, the ever cool never discombobulated bus driver. The trip that generally took forty minutes seemingly had gone by in five. Familiar faces failed to recognize me as I walked through the neighborhood and up the hill home. But Richard Brock would have recognized me with a sack on my head.

"Muse," that's what most of the boys called me, and my brothers too, "what you do with all that hair you had?" While Richard was a sho'nuf case of Pepsi Cola stealing, forever bad mouthin' thug, he always made every effort to display his most gentlemanly ways in my presence. Escorting me home from the bus stop was a social grace he extended whenever he spotted me. Hitting on me or making any kind of untoward advance seemingly never crossed his mind.

"I left it on the bus," I said, smelling my pee and knowing that any such flip thoughts floating through my mind had better vanish by the time I hit that first step at 2424 Second Street.

As I turned the key in the door, I could see my father standing there like he knew I had gone out and done something drastic.

"No, no! What have you gone and done?" as a look of utter amazement, surprise, disgust, and rage came over his face. In 1968, he would go off the deep end again when I got an Afro.

"Where is your hair?" Knowing that the smart-aleck routine was totally unacceptable behavior from me, I couldn't say, "Well, where does it look like it is?" It must have taken me five minutes to swallow the air caught in the rungs of my throat and muster the courage to respond.

"It, iiiiiiiittttt…" Finding the words to form an explanation was like trying to turn a bold-faced lie into a resounding truth.

With tears about to swell in his eyes, Daddy, who seldom shouted at me, was furious. "What in the hell have you done to you hair? Betty, Betty come look at this."

As she turned the corner out of the kitchen into the dining room, her jaw dropped but only halfway. I could have sworn that I saw a wink of approval quickly dart across her face. But Daddy had been wounded, almost mortally. A thing about their daughter's hair sent many a black man of my father's generation into a permanent snit. How dare me, a mere thirteen-year-old, cut my hair into a low-class Bob. As my first real act of parental defiance, it was becoming so uncharacteristically characteristic of me.

That evening, a rare occurrence took place in our household. My father lost his appetite and his great sense of humor, simultaneously. Fletcher Henderson Muse, Sr., looked up at me from his full plate and pushed back from the table saying, "You ruined your hair and my dinner too."

For what seemed like weeks on end he sulked, pouted, and brooded about the loss of my locks. While he pouted, I enjoyed the stabilizing effect of peer acceptance and the new freedom that elevated me above another reason to get my high yella butt kicked.

Now I could jump double-dutch without my braids getting entangled in the rope. Play tennis without one of them wild braids whacking me in the face, run a faster 100-yard dash, and best of all, deal with my darker-skinned female peers on more equal footing.

Barbara Johnson, Alicia Brooks, and the rest of the gang of five were shocked when I showed to school that Friday with my newly coiffed Bob. "Check her out. Went and got your hair cut," noted Barbara with distant approval. "No," I wanted to say, "I had brain surgery." But in a state of trembling confusion I uttered, "It'll help me do better in track."

Touching the smooth line at the nape of my neck Barbara asked, "Who cut your hair?"

"Shirley over on Benning Road," I muttered, minus the confidence that had originally come with the haircut. "You mean yo' momma let's you go on Benning Road? I thought all you yellow girls went to the Cardoza Sisters to get your hair done," she sniped.

Despite the curt remarks, an almost immediate shift took place in our relationship. The bad mad five no longer sneered when they sat next to me in history class, and Barbara Johnson even showed some signs of wanting to build a real friendship with me. At archery practice, she let me go first. Somehow, it was a peculiar kind of affirmation that was one of my early lessons in female bonding.

To a certain degree that Bob liberated me, gave me a stronger sense of myself, and also allowed me to begin forming friendships with girls, some of whom I feared and some of whom I liked. I had to remove a part of myself to gain acceptance from those hershey bar and black velvet girls who had been generationally victimized around skin color. But what could you expect when a fundamental, unwritten social code stipulated that being darker than a paper bag excluded you from certain parties, social sets, jobs, and even friends?

Daphne Muse is a child of the forties who grew up in the fifties, became a civil rights activist in the sixties, traveled the world in the seventies, and has embraced the nineties as the time to honor her spirit and power by wearing her hair as long as it will grow. She is also the author of three children's books and more than one hundred feature articles, review essays, and commentaries on children, youths, and families. Her work has appeared in The Washington Post, Mothering, *and* Konceptualization Jazz Magazine. *She recently completed* The Palace of Honey Heights, *a young-adult novel about a ten-year-old girl's efforts to understand the frustration, pain, and rage that destroyed her South Central Los Angeles neighborhood during the 1992 rebellions.*

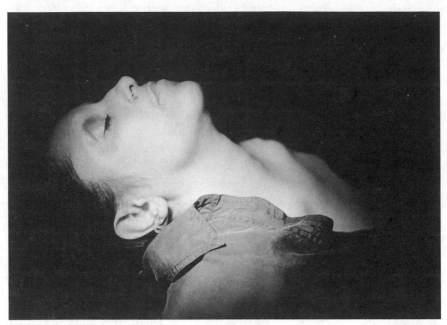

Anita Poree, 1992

Crossing Lines

Anita Poree

> I am 100%
> Of EVERYTHING that I am,
> Choctaw,
> African,
> French,
> Spanish,
> Jew...
> ...and this is very hard for me to say.
> —*Passing for Me*, Anita Poree

On Dad's Side:

At long last, a thought to be my lost uncle of mine was found. For years he was talked about in hushed tones as having disappeared, but at gut understanding was known to have crossed over the color line. Louisiana-born, Dominican-lineaged Creole, camouflaged as a New York Italian. He resurfaced aged, ill, under threat of numbered days and backpacking decades of petrified family bitterness and banishment...

Some crossings go down in cold isolation and very hard.

Then there was the *cousen*, who with a disassociative point of her finger, rerouted my confused, feelings-hurt little brother away from the front door to the back entrance when he dropped by to say hi on his way home from school. And gawd forbid he should slip and hug her or call her by a kinship name, especially when she kept doubling back and forth 'cross that perilous line of schizophrenic identity...

Some crossings get crazy-making.

Yet another *cousen* married Italian and raised her children one-sidely so—only to have to come tiptoeing back to *ma tant* and her fixed income for a loan to ease their humiliating neediness, to keep a roof over their "white" heads...Sometimes crossings impale pride.

And on these stories go, from this side.

On Both Sides:

My family's list of passing or whiting-up is very complex indeed. It bleeds long and longer, dried on past trails of denial and pain. Yet, still

133

bleeding profusely, today it branches and detours hollowed out by old shamings and the scare of fatal backlash. The fear of white stigmas on Black, Red, Brown, Yellow, and the accompanying punishments for displaying these "taints," caused this incessant unhealed bleeding from self-inflicted wounds of betrayal.

Remolding ourselves into the image and likeness of acceptable "minority," for barbed tokens, hurts.

"Better" job security and promotion potential…

"Better" education options…

"Better" housing in seemingly "better" neighborhoods…

"Better" sociopolitical opportunities…

"Better" insurance rates…

"Better"…etc., etc., etc…are not *passe pour blanc* goals of the past. Their rewards are but placebos that minimize our Black, Red, Brown, Yellow selves. They are poisoned teething rings offered up by the Amer-mainstream. Passing and/or whiting up are realities with us now. Wearing illusion masks of melting-pot equality, dazzling us with multicultural quick fixes. We are playing with very dangerous survival toys in the condemned cradles of racism.

On Mom's Side:

The deadly kiss of survival is a legacy imprinted indelibly on my cultural memory. One piece of its mangling puzzle is told in the vicious tug o' war between basic subsistence and serious malnutrition. It was during the Depression where the battle waged, got uglier daily. My grandmother was struggling to feed, educate, and clothe five out of twelve offspring still at home. The family contorted in survival, tried to make ends meet with the pathetic, degrading wage Granddad brought home. A dejected, dispossessed Afro-Indian man. A once-proud farmer, indiscriminately relocated, along with his family, from fertile Muskogee allotment acreage to hammering cattle to death in the Chicago stockyards.

Grandmother decided to pass for white in order to work as a scab seamstress in a garment factory sweatshop. Crossing lines of fiercely threatening strikers; crossing lines of fiercely threatening racists; crossing lines of color to survive fiercely threatening possibilities of homelessness. Her mantra, her battle cry was, "They can't kill us all." Thus this Choctaw woman, with Jewish blood, crossed over and did her workday white routine in order to cope with the madness of poverty and prejudice. In the mornings she and her daughters would ride the rank, smelling, clanging, rocking "el" train together, she in the direction of work and they in opposite directions. Her daughters were beautiful golden and brown Afra-Indians. Sitting apart from them on the rattling old car, Grandmother could not, would not speak to them, show any sign of acknowledgment or affection…mustn't be associated in any way with her own children for fear of being recognized as a woman of color and losing her job. This soul-ripping game of rejection for core survival just about exploded her heart. Its insidiousness became an unresolved, long-standing, deeply hooked-on parasite, segmented in hurt, fear, resentment, grief, and secrets. Feeding upon itself, eating away at her Self. She died too early of this eaten-away condition. "They" called it cancer, but I call it death by forced line crossings.

I will not forget…

Anita Poree is an artist, composer, and writer of Creole and Choctaw ethnicity. She also facilitates sessions for corporations on diversity issues and leads outdoor adventure programs (climbing and backpacking) for self-empowerment.

Diaspora Salvadoreña / Salvadoran Diaspora

Martivón Galindo

Esta es la hora de la huída
abanadona Judea
escapa hacia Egipto
Honduras es campo minado
Guatemala es el otro ejército
México, directo al Hotel Ontario
si probas ser torturado
or revoluciionario exilado
y te pondrán vigilantes en las puertas
y devorará tus entrañas
la soledad en español

Quinientos mil ilegales
todos salvadoreños
que problema Norte América
cuando a la anfitriona libertad
se le apagó la llama
y la cinta está atascada:
"Bienvendios emigrantes
de todas las tierras y razas..."
necesidad había de gente
pero europeos muy blancos...

Refugiados somos dentro de la patria
refugiados dentro de cercos de púas
refugiados dentro de iglesias
cual fieras en montes y cuevas
dentro de la casa sin voz y ventanas

Huyen los sembradores de maíz
del fuego a las cuidades
a volverse estatuas de sal porque insisten
en mirar artás al cantón
y al rancho de paja
huyen buscando los campos hondureños

van a la frontera catracha-guanaca
donde batallones de niños imberbes
hacen de ellos *sandwich* de huesos y carne
o los encierran en jaulas
sin ver ya jamás su milpa y su casa

!Salvadoreños! trashumantes, !huyendo!
refugiados con la patria a cuestas yendo
Volvamos los quinientos mil "ilegales"
de norete muy repuestos
Volvamos los refuigiados en Honduras
Guatemala y México
Volvamos los aislados en silencio
y frío de Canadá
los angustiados solitarios de Europa
Volvamos gigantesca columna
de salvadoreños dispersos

A ver si así, fuerza de mas compacta
todos guanacos refugiados arrechos
recuperamos lo nuestro
y se acaba por siempre esta diáspora.

Now is the hour to flee
abandon Judea, escape to Egypt
Honduras is a minefield
Guatemala has another army
In Mexico you can check into the
          Hotel Ontario
if you can show that you've been tortured
or are a revolutionary in exile
and they'll put guards at the door for you
 and loneliness will tear out your guts
in Spanish, amidst your own race

Half a million illegals,
all Salvadorans
al Americans
what a problem for the USA!

when they put out Liberty's flame
and scratch away her inscription
"Give me your tired, your poor, you
        huddled masses..."
But that was when the country needed people
I mean, Europeans, white folks.

We are refugees inside our own country
refugees inside barbed wire fences
refugees inside churches
as if we were wild beasts in forests and caves
inside the house without voice or windows

The planters of corn now take flight to
        the cities
and turn into pillars of salt, for looking back
toward home
They flee to the Honduran border
where armies of beardless boys
turn them into sandwiches of meat and bones
or put them in cages
where they will never see home again

Salvadorans! migrants, refugees of the world,
        fleeing, fleeing
Let's return, we half a million "illegals"
Let's return those trapped in Canada's
        cold silence
Let's return, the lonely ones in Europe
Let's return, a gigantic column
of dispersed Salvadorans
to see if in that way, with closed ranks,
all we "guanacos" refugees
can recover what's ours
and forever end this diaspora.

Martivón Galindo is a Salvadoran poet, her poems and stories have been published in El Salvador and the United States. She has lived in the San Francisco Bay Area for 12 years.

Neighbors

Linda Noel

The blonde headed boy
Across the road
runs the length
Of half the field & yells
To his mother
Waiting
On her cement steps
   THEY AREN'T HOME

Voices shout me
To attention when
The mother replies
   ASK THE INDIANS

My father stands
On our front porch
As I approach the old Ford
Truck
The boy looks at us
Looks back at his mother
Both look back at us
All stalled

It must be serious
They have come to us
In desperation
The last resort
But we don't take time
To think all that
As the boy crosses
Asphalt halfway
And says
His brother has cut himself
They need a ride
To the hospital

We do not hesitate
To help and haul
The mother holding the flesh
Together of the child
Who has fallen on a canning jar

The gap is wide
And long across the pale
Lean chest

The hospital is cleansed
With silence
It is strange
Sitting near these kids
Who are my neighbors
These frightened strangers

Fear my eyes
And speak no words

Everyone rustles
Through leafs of long ago
Magazines

I ask their names
Finally one answers
Another whispers
And another

They don't ask mine
I wonder if they know
The name of neighbors
They never speak
Of us with names
Just THE INDIANS
Called THE INDIANS
like our mail read
MR & MRS INDIAN
who had INDIAN BOYS
And INDIAN GIRLS

As in
    IT'S IN THE INDIAN'S YARD
    HERE COME THE INDIANS
    OH NO THE INDIANS
    HEY INDIAN
    HOW INDIAN

    HEY WHITE BOY

Stretches silence
All the way to this square
Space
We share while waiting
For the mother
Or someone
Anyone
To bring word
Would he be ok
Would it be long
Should I wait
Does she want me to
Need me to
Fear me too like
Her anxious children
Churning their hands
They hold themselves tight
Until the mother returns
With the stitched child

Everyone is relieved
The ride home on back roads
to my father MR. INDIAN
Waiting on the porch
We all agree gladness
That he wasn't hurt badly
Glad we could help

The children
Scramble behind
Their mother for safety

She thanks us
Offers gas money

We insist it has nothing
to do with money

They turn and walk
The length of asphalt
Back to their house
Without asking
Or speaking our names

Linda Noel: "*I am always amazed to be here. My people survived the California gold rush. I consider myself evidence of miraculous endurance. Concow-Maidu is my tribe. I have done and been many things in my time, and always the most valued is my writing.*"

When we talk about diversity I think it is important to remember that every group counts, we cannot leave anyone out.

—Cherie R. Brown, National Coalition Building Institute

In order to begin the healing process, there must be an admittance of a problem. It is not just Native people that need to heal. The perpetrators of the violence also need to heal…Until we start to see the beauty in the colors that represent our cultures, there will not be peace. We all need to realize the gift of life, we all need to be free.

—Ruth Denny, "Growing Up Indigenous in America"
(*The Circle*, 1992)

No, I Am Not a Vet

(for Charmaine)
A. A. Hedge Coke

Closing, closing long, still,
desperately   trying to rest
my eyes   my visionary
statement   rise
there arises   times
clips, flicks, changes
in time   slipping
back   in time   back
false   film effect
strobe   I see
I remember white
men   white, white
men killing women   and
children   killing Indians
and men   Indian men
trying desperately   to
kill me   our own
men   reacting reaction
action to oppressed
oppression repetitive
it   throws back my
face my heart   slides
down and forth up my
bladed back and crawls
up scratched parched
listless tongue screaming
so silently
quickening relapse tendencies
"But I didn't do anything."
and they proceed to
maim   killing thousands
hundreds, and turn
back on   one   the survivors

this precise second   in
replay   evolves repeating
dream   blows to
the frontal plane
guard my 3-D existence
terrorizing women and children
bayonets slicing   into
tiny warm bodies
beaded flags on
sacred heads   and wisdom
all ages   in their beautiful
black eyes   turning over
and back   in regard to
overwhelming constant
batter and mix whip
lash   to certain refrain
feel the dangling
effect of rabbit punch
to rubber   punching bag
my head   my point
conceptual   conception
thought process shield
and emergence place
I feel you reaching
through   aiming not
at me but deeper
through—behind me
to the wall you
collide   your jabs and
hooks into my skull
protruding damage
through   object resting
above my bladed back
neck snap cheekbone
thrash   eyes no longer
have clean form but
swell beyond recognition
senseless I am suspended
yet standing   out cold
yet balanced on locked
knees   as you   purse   your

reaction action   to the oppression

bestowed upon us
as a people   your anger
and confusion   at images
infants and women
our grandparents   and theirs
being mutilated   and so
you mutilate the mother
of your children
the grandmother of your grandchildren
and drop the bomb—oppression
upon her   that is

was me breaking parts
spirit   breaking my
spirit irreparably for
as long as I exist

*A. A. **Hedge Coke** is Huron, Tsalagi, French Canadian, and Portuguese. This piece was written while in attendance MFA Summer Program Naropa, July 7, 1992 which focused on the Quincentennial issue. Only four Native Americans, four African Americans, two Hispanics, and one Asian were in attendance at this gathering. "Let the work speak for itself."*

Rita Williams

The Custom of the Times

Rita Williams

Clarence Thomas could be family. He speaks in that stilted way of black men under pressure from without and within. The taut cords in his jaw are the same as those in the picture of my uncle. And though I have never met either man, both their stories have much the same tenor.

When my uncle was a slave, he was whipped by his white owner until his skin cracked. He was then bathed in a brine of salt and pepper like a corned beef. According to his memories, "It was thought that the colored race needed no more care than a hog or a cow, and got considerably less than a horse. It was merely the custom of the times. These conditions were so, not because my master was especially cruel, for he was not."

When the Civil War broke out, my uncle joined the Union Army. Eventually he became wealthy, living out the last of his eighty-nine years with my aunt on a 3,000-acre ranch in Nebraska. Nowhere in his story does he express any bitterness over having been tortured. This mystifies me—I know many people who have suffered considerably less than he did who are crippled by their rage. But I withhold judgment because the great accomplishment is that his memoirs were written at all. I do know this: anger has to go somewhere.

I have been raised to view men like Clarence Thomas much the same as a priest or the president. These male and distant leaders function like the lead goose, flying first into the wind to create a break for the chevron coming behind. They may be one-dimensional, but their role is that of leader. Virtue is not an issue. In turn, these men feel entitled to a mute woman. It's like the father in *Boyz N the Hood* who says of his ex-wife that if she hadn't talked so much, she could have kept him. The man is the prize—women just have to be silent.

In 1922, after my uncle had established his ranch, he went south to find a wife. Love and romance were not even remote considerations. It was an exchange of goods and services. My aunt was twenty-one when she met this man in his seventies who had more money than she knew existed. He opened the world to her. He brought her entire family up from Arkansas. But although I never heard her say so, the price she paid was powerful. One night she told me, "My husband and I were sitting on the porch one evening, and he remarked about my mama's long hair. I told him she was a Cherokee, and he said they had a hard time during the war."

"One night he told me how he'd been walking along a ridge just after dusk. The bright moon fully lit the cottonwoods which were starting to turn, but the valley was in shadow. He looked down in the ravine, and yonder was an old squaw. She had a little girl with her, couldn't have been more than three or four. And the squaw was digging worms with a stick and feeding them to the child, because they was starving. His regiment had been told to kill all the Indians they came upon, on sight. But he said she was just too poor. He just didn't have the heart to kill that one."

"So he left them alone and just went on back to his regiment and didn't tell nobody. Said he never spoke of it again until the night he told me. See, they recruited the colored regiment to kill the Indians."

I became incensed when I heard those words "that one," but I knew I dare not question her or demand to know more. She was loyal, and if questioned directly with any show of emotion, would clam up. Still, the questions rankle. What happened to this woman and her child? What happened to the other Cherokees?

The first time my aunt spoke to me of these things, she was ninety-one years old. As she sat before me, I saw the high cheekbones and arched nose of the Cherokee. She had no idea what she had said, or rather, what I had heard. Certain murders you must come to accept.

After the Civil War, my uncle came west to work on the ranch of one of the greatest of the old cattle barons, a man who had murdered not only Native Americans, but any white men who impeded the massive cattle drives. But the baron would fire any cowpoke he caught speaking profanity, and if you worked for him, you went to church on Sunday. My uncle was glad to have a job.

I realize I must face fully that my uncle, this Civil War veteran, was a part of all this. And certainly like many of this country's heroes, he committed murder. For what mattered then was what white men thought important. Certainly, the experience of women and blacks didn't count, and even if they had spoken out, there was no one in the land to hear them.

Then, as now, any woman speaking of her own sexuality wasn't considered worthy of respect, and a woman speaking of a man's sexuality was a downright traitor. As with those murders, these things were done but not discussed. (All this is doubly complicated by the delicacy, vulnerability, and sanctity of sexual intimacy, which should not be for public consumption.) One night, however, my aunt did speak. "My wedding night, I was so scared I hid in the closet. He come and got me. He ripped off my gown and said, "From now on, you'll do as I tell you." After that, I got used to it."

Then she laughed, went on matter-of-factly to speak of their travels together, his teaching her to write a check, her enormous sense of loss when he died in a car accident. And given where she came from, the child of a sharecropper, one of thirteen, his gifts to her *were* enormous. At a time when black men and women were slightly less valuable than horses, if she had chosen to speak, she would have sacrificed the greatest opportunity she had ever had. But I have to face the fact that not only was this man a murderer, he was also a rapist.

My uncle ends his memoirs with these words: "After all is said and done, I find that there is no greater rule for making and holding friends, for happiness and contentment and real enjoyment of life, than in doing unto others as I would like them to do unto me, and try to do it just a little better."

Like Clarence Thomas at the beginning of the hearings, my uncle writes with reverence of the inconceivable distance both he and his beloved America had traveled since his birth. He is not troubled by his past, and he would be highly insulted at my uppitiness in examining his life. He would look at the advantages I have been given and consider me too spoiled and too shallow to judge him. He was doing what he felt was necessary to overcome inconceivable deprivation.

But the deadliest lies are the ones in which all of us, black and white, male and female, collude in deceiving ourselves. So, for me, the wonder is not the detail of Anita Faye Hill's allegations, nor the fact that she spoke so late, but the fact that she dared to speak at all.

Who can ever know with absolute certainty whether Thomas harassed her? The most conservative people I know were at one time outsiders standing with their noses pressed to the glass, hoping against hope that one day they would be invited in. Clarence Thomas, like my uncle, doesn't want to demolish the reigning order. He just wants a piece of the plantation.

Rita Williams, a recovering Catholic African/Jewish Native American, is a free-lance writer living in Los Angeles. In 1992, her work appeared in several national anthologies: Lovers; Catholic Girls *and* Psychological Perspectives. *She was also published in* Transition, the International Review of Postcolonial People. *A short story will be coming out this year in* Catholic Girls and Boys. *She is currently working on a novel about her family of African-American hunting guides in the Rocky Mountains in the 1930s entitled* Wild Women of the West.

Racism is pervasive to the point that we take many of its manifestations for granted, believing "that's life." I've run into folks who really think that we can beat this devil, kick this habit, be healed of this disease in a snap. In a sincere blink of a well-intentioned eye, presto—poof—racism disappears. "I've dealt with my racism...(envision a laying on of hands)...Hallelujah! Now I can go to the beach." Well, fine. Go to the beach. In fact, why don't we all go to the beach and continue to work on the sucker over there? Cuz you can't even shave a little piece off the thing called racism in a day, or a weekend, or a workshop.

—Gloria Yamato
"Something about the Subject Makes It Hard to Name"
from *Making Face, Making Soul: Haciendo Caras*

Strange Juice (*The Murder of Latasha Harlins*)

Sapphire

I remember my boyfriend, the dark behind the brown of his eyes and how he look in his leather. I was walking with that good feeling, thinking about him, the next day of school—maybe I go, maybe I don't. You know who gives a fuck. And nothing special; you know nothing is so special except now I'm dead. It's the day I died. And the sky was red-brown gauze. You could see patches of blue if you look up but I don't hardly ever look up. My eyes on the ground feeling my feet in Orange Reeboks. What else I remember? Now that I look back it seems like the collard greens piled up on the plywood boards at the door was huge green tears that sought to warn me. The day was the same. Different. I didn't do nothin'. I slid open the glass door of the refrigerator that keeps all the beverages cool; it's so hot here. My eyes glance up at the camera pointed like a gun from the corner of the wall. Fuck it. I slip the cold bottle of orange juice in my backpack, go to the counter. I'll get some gum; if she says something I'll say, aw bitch I was gonna buy this juice, you think I'm stupid. Wonder what we gonna do at school tomorrow. I be so glad to get out the ninth grade, go to high school. If I'm late for homeroom one more time…

"Oh bitch please! I was gonna pay for—OOG FU WOO SMIT SUE! Speak English hoe! Take you damn juice. I wasn't stealing nothin' from you chink ass hoe!"

She grabbed me. Bitch! I hit that hoe upside her jaw. Who the fuck she think she is puttin' her hands on somebody. Fuck this hoe, I ain' gon' argue with this bitch. I turn my back. And walk away. I see the collard greens again, only now they're growing like big trees; then I see a red dirt road in the middle of the salad bar, no lie, like I'm high or something. Then everything is normal Koreatown fruit stand again. Del Monte corn out a can poured in a stainless steel tub, iceberg, romaine, bran muffins, and brownies wrapped in clear plastic. Fuck it, I'm not thirsty no way.

> I don't hear the blast till I'm dead
> I don't feel nothin' either
> as I split in half
> a dog yelps
> and every sound I ever heard

flies out my mouth on green wings
and crimson waterfalls open in my skull
and my bones come aloose.
The dog is screaming
like a siren now
and in the distance a bucket of water
spills over a dusty red dirt road
and my heart quits
falls face first in
shattered glass on a
concrete floor.
The camera keeps
rolling.
My left leg twitches.
I don't cry.
Fifteen.
Green as greens
passing from sight
under broken bottles of light.

2.
I don't remember what I did wrong.
somebody hit you, you hit 'em back.
She didn't have to shoot me.
I was born here
and someone can shoot me and go home
and eat turkey on Thanksgiving—
what kind of shit is that?
Videotape the bitch killing me,
the hoe's own videotape recording
the end of my days
reeling obscenely
for T.V. cameras—
my blood
sweet Jesus!
Rolling 20s
Bounty Hunters
PJs
Imperial Courts
NWA
LAPD

South Central
Hollywood
18th Street Diamond Riders
Easy Riders
it's a black thang
it's a brown thang
Crips
Bloods, Mexican together forever tonite.
I don't remember...
I jus' wanted some juice
and now I'm dead.
Killed by a model minority
success story.
Listen, is anybody gonna
say anything?
I was gonna get a new orange leather jacket
to match my Reeboks.
I was passing math *and*
doing good in English.
Fuck history, I'm tired of hearing
bout George Washington
and Columbus.
I told that cracker, "Shit, mutherfucker
what about us?"

No, I wasn't pregnant,
but I was gonna have a baby,
definitely, one day.
I like Luther Vandross, Tone Loc
and Queen Latifa.
Listen, is anybody gonna
say anything?
Community service!
A white bitch
with a pink slit
between her legs
like mine,
drips red.
A white girl that probably got
into law school on the
affirmative action birthed

by black people's struggle,
sitting on a seat
that was opened up
for her by Rosa Parks and
Fannie Lou Hamer
nig—no, black people, African
Americans, like me, marching
under fire, hoses, broken glass
gasolined bodies
testicles sliced off,
strange fruit, tossed to dogs.
Swing from trees.

This white judge woman
hooded in mahogany walled
chambers decides my life
is not worth nothing.
A fifteen year old black girl
equals zero in this white bitch's book.
She sentences this yellow gunslinger
to community service and probation?
What are the terms of her probation?
That she don't kill nobody white?
Does anybody hear me?
Without my tongue.
Fifteen and out of time.
Listen to the gasoline on the wind.
Listen to my blood rhyme
drip drop on the sidewalk.
Hear me children—
and BURN.

Sapphire is a forty-three-year-old African American poet and writer who lives and works in New York City. "Strange Juice" is excerpted from American Dreams: Poetry and Prose, *forthcoming from HIGH RISK Books/Serpent's Tail in Winter 1994.*

The Korean Rap

Holly Yasui

June 23, 1992. With the fires of Los Angeles still searing our memories, we gather to commemorate the murder of Vincent Chin. It's the tenth-year anniversary of that evening when the twenty-seven-year old Chinese American was beaten to death with a baseball bat. Two unemployed auto workers shouted, "It's because of you Japs that we're out of work!" then bashed his head in.

We're at Hing Hay Park in the International District of Seattle. Hing Hay is actually less a park than an urban square. There's no grass, but cobbled pavement, a red-and-gold pagoda shelter, a Chinese mural, and backless wood benches. A couple of years ago, local businesses in the renovated Pioneer Square area militated against the homeless, so street people started migrating toward Occidental Park, then to Hing Hay. Asian, Blacks and Native Americans hang around in Hing Hay, watching tourists snap photos of the picturesque pagoda and mural.

I look at the xeroxed program. *Predictable: "comments" by our Asian American community leaders, student leaders…but what's this? A rap performance by two Koreans students, the Seoul Brothers. That should be something!* I nudge my friend Imelda, point at the program, and joke that they should have put the Seoul Brothers last, as a reward for standing through all the speeches.

Though it's evening, it's very warm. It was over ninety degrees during the day. Windows in the run-down hotels around the square are open and people sitting by them smoke, fan themselves, and gaze at us below.

The program is off to a slow start. The microphone is erratic and it's hard to hear the speakers. I gaze around at the crowd. Chinese, Japanese, Korean, Filipino, Vietnamese, and a few white, brown, and black faces: I'm pleased. Then the Seoul Brothers stride onstage, brash and stylish young hip-hops. I smile, imagining what their parents say to them when they visit home.

The older brother takes the mike and introduces the rap with remarks that wipe the patronizing smile from my lips. "Everybody knows that us Koreans were targeted in the LA riots," he says with some belligerence. *Sister Latasha! This is for Little Sister Latasha!* "But we stood together, to defend ourselves against them!" *The young Korean vigilante, gun in hand, wearing a Malcom X Tee-shirt, by any means necessary…but that was tragic! We are all,*

157

black, yellow, and brown, oppressed by the same dominant power structure.

The immediate insistence of the rap interrupts my thoughts. They're rapping about empowerment, blasting the model-minority stereotype. They're smart and sharp, ebullient and angry. The crowd sways slightly to the beat. I'm conscious of the physical restraint exhibited by this group of Asian Americans, and I feel inhibited. Not only because of Latasha Harlins... *Just don't do anything to draw attention to yourself, sweetheart, and we'll be all right, Mama whispers, and I try to melt into her skirts. She doesn't walk any faster or slower than usual, just normal as if nothing were wrong, and I think she must be the bravest person in the world.*

As the rap warms up, my body remembers other events, when everyone really got up and whooped and hollered and clapped and moved with the music, the message, the mood. *Shit, Mama, all that hiding all those years, your whole life, so well-behaved! haven't you heard the news? It's better to die on your feet than to live on your knees!*

Mama looks at me with alarm. Oh, sweetheart, you don't know what you're saying. We've worked so hard to give you a chance to live a good life. That's all I've ever cared about. Don't you understand, all that noise and shouting is not our way. There are some things that can't be helped. *Shi kata ga nai.* It can't be helped.

Through sudden tears, I notice one of the street people, an old, rail-thin Black man, sauntering over to the stage area. He starts clapping and moving with the rap. He's dipping and swinging, twirling and laughing. I let out a yell and stamp my feet. *It can be helped! It can! We can make music, talk story, and dance together. It's a start, at least it's a beginning!* I think of Emma Goldman who said that she didn't want to take part in the revolution if she couldn't dance...or something like that.

But even as these feelings rise in me, I notice a cop—the one Asian cop, standing off to the side with two white cops—moving toward the stage. He politely takes the dancing man by the arm and starts to walk him out of the stage area. *What's he doing? Why him? Did the white guys put him up to it? Was it his idea? Did he feel proprietary because this is an "Asian" event?* The cop's face is tight, controlled. My immediate reaction is to boo loudly. The women in front of me turn around and whisper, "Shhhhhh!"

"He wasn't disrupting! He was having fun! He was great!" I say to Imelda, who whispers, "I know, I know" in a way that means "be quiet, forget it." The women in front of me turn around again.

"It's rap; he has a right to the stage!" They look at me with that pained expression I used to see so often on my mother's face. Then they turn their backs to me, inched away from me. I can tell that Imelda is embarrassed, wishes that she hadn't come to this event with me.

I could have shouted, "Let him dance!" instead of whispering, but something my mama gave me kept me silent. *We did survive, after all. And we managed to buy some illusion of security by doing things "properly" and working twice as hard for half as much. Like many other people of color. But for some reason, it stuck to us. No one told us that whatever we achieved would be used against us, building this myth of the model minority, to keep us in our place, to breed resentment against us from all sides.*

The program continues, according to the agenda. The recitation of anti-Asian hate crimes roll off the walls of my consciousness. I am trapped in silence, now and when Ms. Du murdered young black Latasha Harlins. When she, like the murderers of Vincent Chin, received probation and a suspended sentence from a white judge.

The girl had money in her hand for the juice she was going to buy when the shopkeeper shot her. Why don't we talk about Ms. Du and Latasha Harlins?

We can't talk about that, because then they'll just say that Japs hate Koreans.

But she murdered a young girl!

You don't understand the cultural differences.

No. No cultural differences justify murder. Maybe she wasn't polite, but that was no reason to kill her.

She panicked.

Who? Latasha Harlins or Mrs. Du?

Forget it, ok? Listen, there's no use in bringing up things that divide us… Don't you know how hard it is to create a Pan-Asian movement? How fragile it still is? And besides, even if it was wrong, it was no excuse for torching Korean shops!

No justice, no peace.

I tell Imelda that I have to go, and we leave Hing Hay Square. The words of the speakers still bruise my mind as the dancing black man is led off by the Asian cop in front of the silent crowd, of which I am a part. *Money in her hand, a bullet in her back…flames engulfing buildings, the streets thick with smoke… How is it that we, people of color who know the pain of exclusion and racism, allow it to happen and even become its enforcers? How better to keep us all in our places?*

No justice, no peace. No peace, no justice. How do we break the cycle?

"Let him dance!" a voice rings out. The cop turns, surprised.

"Let him dance! Let him dance!" Several voices.

"Let him dance! Dance! Let him dance!" Many voices, chanting.

The cop glances at the crowd, then the Korean rappers, who, responding to the crowd, nod and gesture to bring the dancer back. The cop shrugs and releases the man's arm. The dancing man slips under his elbow with a flourish and a cheer goes up in the crowd. The black dancer and the Korean rappers continue, as if made for each other.

By the time it's done, the whole square is tapping and snapping and sweating, including the street people at the margins of the crowd, standing and dancing on the benches. We all applaud each other.

It takes a while for the crowd to quiet down, but as speakers rise to give testimony, the audiences grows quiet, the street people sit on the benches and listen. A woman reads off names: Vincent Chin. Jim Loo. The Vietnamese children at the Stockton schoolyard. In the midst of the litany, someone shouts: What about Latasha Harlins?"

The audience is silent for a brief moment, then stirs. Someone in back claps and shouts, "Justice for all hate crimes!" Others clap, hesitantly at first. "Justice for all!" Then with more vigor: "Justice for all! Justice for all!"

Holly Yasui is a graphic designer and writer, recently moved from Seattle, Washington, to Mexico. Her writing has appeared in the International Examiner, Northwest Ethnic News, Northwest Nikkei, *and* Raven Chronicles. *Her play* Unvanquished *was winner of the 1991 Multicultural Playwrights Festival. She was a resident at Hedgebrook Cottages for Women Writers in 1992 and encourages women of color to investigate this unique residency.*

Sometimes when I was growing up, my identity seemed to hurtle toward me and paste itself right to my face. I felt that way, encountering the stereotypes of my race perpetuated by non-Japanese people (primarily white) who may or may not have had contact with other Japanese in America. "You don't like cheese, do you? someone would ask. "I know your people don't like cheese."

—Kesaya E. Noda, "Growing Up Asian in America"

Part II

On Becoming
*Ad*Normal:
Finding, Creating,
and Accepting Wellness

Exploring ways to create more adnormal—healthy, life-affirming—behavior is the purpose of this section. It is an amalgamation of love, gossip, and wisdom for a community of women who struggle with and thrive amidst the unsanity of America. Women share the tools used to improve and maintain their mental health and well-being in this culture. Speaking truth and reconnecting to our true selves—our Authentic Selves—are essential to our healing from the anti-life, abnormal behaviors fostered by American culture. Staying vigilant and rooting out the poisons within, accepting imperfection (your own and that of others), remaining vulnerable and being able to embrace the miracle of shared humanity are central to individual and collective adnormalcy.

Healing, while a very personal process, requires the support of a loving, caring community. Working toward wellness together is the beginning of alliance-building in your own life and community. Alliance-building is not just a healing, but the beginning of a political process that gives us the empowerment of numbers to address the inequity and injustice that are so often responsible for discontent, denial, disease, and death in the lives of women of color. Spirit is not separate from politics.

Remember as you read to strive for what Alice Walker called "the best Self." Know the best Self is there, the Authentic Self is there, and try to achieve it.

Genny Lim

The Wildness of Women

Genny Lim

Cut out their tongues and make them talk
Strip off their clothes and make them walk
down by the village in the river of blood
Feel the heat, feel the fire, feel the flood
Feel the flames, feel the wind and the mud
My backbone rising, rising
from the jungle of my groins, the dark of my circle
From the roots of my forest, to the dark fruit of
my nothing, nothing, nothing-ness

The Wildness of Women
is irreversible
The Doubleness of Women
is diabolical
The price of the market has no value
when women give voice
their god is devalued
Ah, now you see, now you don't
Ay yes, Life, Ay no, Death
The women have the power to cure and kill
The women call the powers that touch and thrill
The mountain spirits, the flight of birds
The water spirits, the forest herbs
The jungle of man's fear is
mirrored in a woman's tears
With feathers and mirrors
She kills, she cures

The Wildness of Women
is unpredictable
The magic of women
is unimaginable
Visions of thought made real
Women washing gold in lakes

Women spinning space between their legs
Women spewing words in waterfalls
Ah, now you see, no you don't
life, now you see, Death, now you don't
Ay yes, Life, ay no, Death
The women have the power to cure and kill
the women have the power to touch and thrill
The mountain spirits, the flight of birds
The water spirits, the forest herbs
The jungle of man's fear is
mirrored in a woman's tears
With feathers and mirrors
She kills, she cures

Cut out our tongues and make us talk
Strip off our clothes and make us walk
down by the village in the river of blood
Feel the feat, feel the fire, feel the flood
Feel the flames, feel the wind, feel the mud
Feel our backbones rising, rising up
from the jungle of our groins, the dark of our circles
from the roots of our forest,
from the dark fruit of our souls

You come to us—Why?
to be cured or feared?
You come to us—Because you love us or
Because you hate us?
You come to us in
an endless caravan of horses and people
With hooves and feet
drumming across the bridge of fate
Across the Pacific, across the peaks of mountains
and foothills and rainforests
through green valleys and quiet deserts
With your guns and your prayers
There is no refuge, there is no cure—no milagro
from the Book of Magic, the Book of Magia

Rosemary, Romero for insomnia and nightmares
Marigold for inflammation

Garlic for infections
Quina for baldness
Chinaroot for kidneys
Chamomile for digestion
Rhubarb for diarrhea
Ginseng to stimulate the blood
Paradero to stimulate fertility
Tuercemadre to inhibit fertility
Bearfat for rheumatism
Spingo for nerves
Altamisa for exorcisms (Casa Salada—a bewitched house)
A rabbit's foot for good luck

But there is no cure, no cure for
the sorcery of modern madness
For the magic of corporate technology
for the filth of chemical creations
is irreversible
The greed of conquest
is insatiable
The power of wealth
is demonic

Cut out our tongues, strip off our clothes
We will talk, We will walk
Into the villages, with blood on our skins
With the fire, with the flood
With the wind, with the mud
Our backbones rising, rising
From our hearts, from our groins
With feathers, mirrors, candles and bells
We shall kill and we shall cure

Genny Lim is a Chinese American native San Franciscan poet and playwright. Her plays include Angels, Bitter Cane, XX, *and* La China Poblana. *She is also the coauthor of* Island: Poetry and History of Chinese Immigrants on Angel Island, 1910–1940, *and a collection of poems,* Winter Place. *An award-winning performing poet, her frequent music and poetry collaborations include musicians Jon Jang, Max Roach, Francis Wong, and Herbie Lewis.*

Truth Telling

Joy James

A certain level of honesty should be the ground on which we stand. That involves the pain of truth telling, even saying things to each other that appear to be divisive. Being honest with each other is very much a matter of revealing our flaws and telling the ways in which we rub each other the wrong way so that we can fit together as a community

Part of the truth telling is, for me, that the crucial issue remains "race." Of course, sexuality, class, gender, and religion are all important components of our present social conditions, but I believe that race will be the crucial issue as we enter the twenty-first century as it continues to shape our sexual, class, and gender experiences.

If we look globally at the destruction of community and the disappearance of cultures, this process very much remains racialized, and that is part of our inheritance. So if we are to function as a community, I would like to see us challenge that inheritance in a very radical fashion. That means not only that we need to develop sharper critiques of racism and white supremacy, and the ways in which they assault every community in every culture and all women, but that we also need to challenge caste systems that exist among ourselves. This requires that we have a loving commitment to radicalism. I am committed to ruthless struggle, but I don't want to become so committed that I forget the humane side. I try to remember that radical change, or the uprooting process, is not about controlling anything.

When I have political fights with other women about racism, it is sometimes very hard to remember that we all belong to one human community. The sheer arrogance and insolence I encounter amazes me sometimes, and the only way I can keep from being overwhelmed by bitterness and from refusing to join in communities with women "as women" is by going back to an idea of struggle where love is the center. But that doesn't mean taking abuse from people. It means that you tell the truth no matter what, and you struggle with such principle that you never allow yourself to disrespect your opponent's humanity. You have to repsect your opponent's humanity; you remain linked to her or him.

I have found that, while it is easy to dismiss my opponent's humanity and use that heightened anger and that "moral justification" to push things through, anger is not the best energy to work with if it doesn't have a loving perspective. You can be just as principled by accepting the humanity of people who are destructive, who are arrogant, who act as if they were born to rule, while opposing that kind of behavior by the strength that loving gives you, if you can tap into it.

A very important aspect of the idea of community is that you can't learn this loving in isolation. You really can only learn this kind of loving when it is not easy. It is almost as if through struggle you learn love that is reconciliation without acquiescence. This requires understanding the lay of the land and then doing what is necessary to change the terrain, to change the landscape and make it more habitable for human beings.

A women's community apart from the community at large is a social construction that can become a retreat. Women who feel that they have nowhere else to go may not challenge each other, in order not to lose the only community they have. One cannot form anything truly revolutionary in the communities' outlook and loving in the most uncompromising fashion, out of desperation or retreat. You would compromise to maintain that association or "community."

Our political ideologies as women reflect the span of political ideologies in this society, from Nazi to progressive revolutionary. I am very careful where I walk and with whom I form coalitions or community. The point is not to lose your energy in trying to sustain something that may not have roots, that may be like weeds growing with very shallow roots.

This culture is becoming increasingly violent, and I see our choices narrowing. It is a matter of getting to our feet and acting quickly because there is less leeway and less time to make mistakes. And in this process, women will self-select. Not every woman or every group of women will find that the benefits of a democratic space outweigh the elitist privileges they get from climbing a little higher up in the hierarchies of society.

What is rooted, what grows deep, will transcend women's community. All our different cultures and spiritual practices speak to what that community is. It is a community that transcends gender and all the different ways in which we have been socialized to think in compartments.

Joy James, co-editor of Spirit, Space, and Survival, African American Women in White Academe *(forthcoming from Routledge), teaches womanist theory and courses on African American women and liberation movements at the University of Massachusetts at Amherst.*

Spiritual Attunement in a Secular World

Karla Jackson-Brewer

Western technocratic society would have us all believe the myth that you succeed in this life by your own brute strength, hard work, and willpower. We are encouraged to regard those who achieve success as being intrinsically worthy and good, regardless of how they attained that success. We are indoctrinated with the idea of individualistic success from an early age. The ability to be self-focused, self-involved, and self-centered, at the expense of others, is prized within the competitive, capitalistic system. In school we learn the values projected by society, and we are also taught to respond to rational, linear thought, to consider it the supreme mode of expression. All other modes are discouraged and devalued, and finding the correct answer becomes more important than the process used to obtain that answer. Patriarchal, sexist, and racist society has placed some people in a position of advantage while simultaneously discarding others as unproductive, valueless beings. Women and people of color are always competing, in spite of themselves, from a disadvantaged position.

This myth of the successful, competitive individual runs counter to the natural desire of human beings to work collectively and in community. It leaves no room for a spiritual path or a spiritual life. So much energy is focused outward, by design, that there is little time left of inner-focused, receptive, nonlinear thought. The struggle to live as a spiritual person on a spiritual path is thus a formidable one.

Living in New York City provides me with a vantage point from which to see how popular culture, secularity, and competition hypnotize people into a trance of "not enough, no time." The pull of this stream of popular culture leaves us hungry, unsatisfied, and yearning to have more. People of color in New York find that they are excluded from much of mainstream society in very real and important ways, and participation in that society becomes a constant lure just outside their reach. In neighborhoods with substandard housing, fewer city services, poverty, poorly functioning schools, high unemployment, drug wars, addiction, and greater police presence, the attitude of indifference generated from outside these communities fosters indifference within them. Living not far from some of the wealthiest and most achievement-oriented people in the country encourages us to enter into a treadmill existence of chasing the golden carrot in an atmosphere of disempowerment, disenfranchisement, and defeat.

As a Black woman, I find that the daily distractions of urban living, family needs, professional responsibilities, and other demands on my time often take precedence over my own spiritual needs. I collapse at the end of the week wondering why I live my life in such a frenzied way.

Then I remember to meditate. I do the Dakini Practice (a Tantric Buddhist practice that employs the use of visualization in meditation of a powerful and sometimes wrathful female deity) and feel the energy flowing back into my body. I become again cognizant and mindful of my purpose in life. The Dakinis represent the eternal flow of energy and can be called upon to remove obstacles and clarify dualistic visions. They are the most important manifestation of the feminine in Tibetan Buddhism.

My path of spiritual evolution has been a winding road. In retrospect I see the spiral of my spiritual connection spinning, ever-growing, centering as I take each step into my spiritual power. It has not been an easy path. I am often filled with doubts about the direction I must take or the validity of my intuition. Once I reflect or clear myself with my spiritual rituals, I am able to be still with the oneness of my soul's essence, my ancestors, my spirit guides, and the universe.

The struggle to find and maintain a spiritual path is both rewarding and frustrating. As a Black woman, I was born into the herstory of a people familiar with the world of the unseen, the world of animistic and anthropomorphic magic. In this world, ancestors visit in dreams and visions, spirits speak in the wind, and objects hold the energy of environments and people. Information can be readily accessed by those who have developed the ability to see and hear through the veil that separates the worlds. The Wisdom Energies, the spirits of deities, ancestors, and loved ones, exist only to serve and assist us in our spiritual evolution. Acceptance of the idea that these spirits are with us and faith in the possibility of a better existence provided my ancestors with the strength to survive slavery. This same acceptance fosters the strength within me to continue living as a spiritual being in an environment that operates to deceive and destroy my spiritual light.

I have developed a spiritual way of living that reflects much of how I am as a Black woman and draws upon the many spiritual beliefs of people of color. I am drawn to spiritual practices, perhaps from an earlier life, that resonate within me. I attempt to reclaim the woman-centered spirituality that has been taken from me by patriarchy. Rituals that include water, herbs, and crystals, chanting, smudging, the use of dance, drumming, and sound, have been incorporated into my life. As I explore African, Asian, and Native American spiritual traditions, rituals, and teachings, I am awed by the commonalities that exist among them and the familiarity I feel with them. I honor the spiritual practices of all people, and I believe that with respect for their differences I can evolve through some of these practices. It is also important for me to discover images, archetypes, and practices that reflect my phenotypic physical expression in this life—my African origin.

I was always aware of the part of me that was unacceptably assertive, centered, and strong-willed. I learned, at an early age, that a Black female child should not be too confident in a patriarchal world that is both racist and sexist. I learned to become afraid of the power that existed in me, and I saw few models of powerful Black women around me. I attempted to hide the confident, powerful aspects of my being behind a shield of accommodation, although I had already convinced myself on another level that I really wasn't powerful at all. I wanted to believe that there were strong, powerful women in the world, but I had no concrete evidence that they existed.

As a child I was an avid reader of fantasy and mythology. I turned to these stories in search of metaphors for my development and my life. I discovered the Goddess, and in her discovered many archetypes for my womanpower. I learned to draw on the energy of the Earth and the powerful cultural and ancestral beings who were waiting to assist me on the path to spiritual empowerment and enlightenment. All I had to do was ask for their help and surrender to their guidance. I then felt supported and knew in every cell in my being that I was not alone. I am thankful for the goddesses Isis, Yemaya, Oshun, Oya, Kali, Tara, the Dakinis, and others who have manifested in my life, calling out the many aspects of my being.

The universe is truly responsive to our needs; we only need to be open to what is offered. As I became more aware of my true spiritual nature, other women—particularly women of color—presented themselves in my life. These women acted as guardians and guides on my spiritual path. They reflected for me various aspects of spiritual expression and established the sense of community that I so greatly needed. We shared spiritual practices and information and became witness to each others' evolution.

We nurtured ourselves in Afrocentricity, claiming the images that provided the metaphors for our lives. We connected to and centered ourselves in our African history, ancestors, and aesthetics. We were empowered by all of those African sisters who governed, healed, created, and "stepped out of line," the women who defied the prescribed role for women, flourished, survived, and become heroes within the limitations of that role. Those women, in the present and the past, assist us in creating our metaphors; and our love of our African nature, the spirit of survival and beauty, continues to feed our souls. We learned to laugh, cry, sing, and dance together. We took leadership from one another and responded to the intuitive information that Spirit presented. We created rituals for our healing and for our celebration, and I learned that I could be vulnerable and strong, moving and receptive, silent and powerful. I learned to weave my spiritual practices into a cloak of protection and power, assuring my success against the forces of the seductive illusions of the secular world.

My spiritual development places me in the present, which is indubitably the position of greatest power. I am no longer compelled to take responsibility for other people's reactions to me. I am, however, responsible for the ethical use of the power that grows within me. By listening to and trusting in my intuition and my spirit guides, I continue to spin the true light energy of my being. Spiritual attunement is lifelong activity that for me, as a Black woman, empowers myself and my community, while it honors my ancestors. It is possible to live and walk a spiritual path in the midst of chaos and ignorance. The more I employ and trust my spiritual path, the more able I am to resist the energy-sapping stream of the secular world. My spiritual work connects me to the life-supporting nature of the universe, and by attuning to that I can achieve success that is full, whole, and supports all sentient beings.

Karla Jackson-Brewer is an African American woman who lives on the Lower East Side of New York City with her three children: Jamal, fifteen; Sadira, seven; and Dakota, twenty-seven months; and her husband Garry. Karla is a feminist psychotherapist in private practice working primarily with sexual assault survivors. She is an adjunct professor of Women's Studies and African Studies at Rutgers University. She is also exploring African and Native American traditions of spirituality.

Nora Hall

Attending to Process

Nora Hall

Imagine participating in a community—by which I mean all kinds of groups including families, clubs, and neighborhoods—that easily works through conflicts and efficiently channels differing agendas into large-scale goals that serve a diverse populace. Imagine a highly productive collective whose goals are not bogged down because of clashes from political groups representing different historical experiences, varying values, needs, and interests.

These situations are especially accessible to women because we have experienced inequality and are beginning to understand diversity among feminists.

When women come together, our shared experience of having some aspect of our identity imposed and constructed by society and the differences between our experiences—political, philosophical, class-related, spiritual, or otherwise—often appear at odds. While women instinctively understand the experience of being a collective, the clash of experiences makes it difficult and sometimes impossible to develop progressive communities.

Women often fail to draw upon our social histories for invaluable information about the role of power in society. Women's shared social history provides the center that we need to assist the process work of groups. Conflicts, no matter how small the stakes, are the product of power struggles. They are struggles between the powerful and the disempowered and as such may be viewed as both obvious and perceived elements of group process.

Women know a great deal about the power struggles inherent in group processes because we have experienced various forms of oppression and inequality within society. Some women may have even more perspective on specific elements of process because of race/ethnicity, class, or sexual orientation, which give rise to dual or triple-edged oppressions.

Most people view process as a waste of time rather than seeing the work as an empowering tool for group transformation. Today's complex organizations rely on leaders who can effectively guide group progress and manage the stress that is essential to a community's growth. The future promises to be even more complicated, requiring organizers and group leaders to have highly sophisticated skills.

If present demographic trends continue, community diversity will increase greatly by the year 2000. The term "diversity" is used to denote gender difference, class distinctions, sexual orientation, racial/ethnic difference, other identities, as well as individual and factional differences within a collective that has a common group identity, for example, women. Such change is likely to create a great many community conflicts over resources, goals, policies, procedures, and any number of related issues.

Given our roles as survivors, women are the perfect group to build strong collectives that call for a high sensitivity to process. Enabling diverse groups of people to work together in the future will require organizers who emphasize group process as a leadership tool. Keen insight about what is necessary for diverse groups to work together will be a key component, as will the ability to respond to different historical experiences and values.

In many cases, when conflicts arise in women's organizations, the stakes many seem small by societal standards. But the casualties are ordinary people who have very little power, and people are not minor stakes no matter what their societal status. Insensitivity to human resources prevents many leaders from developing the process skills that are necessary to support and enhance vital community resources.

A major challenge for women in the future will be dealing with the process of power in women's communities. Many women do not see themselves as powerful even when they are entrusted with leadership. In a similar vein, other women may not view the leader as powerful or important, thus undermining her leadership. These processes are by-products of women's socialization, but if they go unchallenged, they can seriously hamper a community's growth.

Nora Hall is a writer, educator, and organizational consultant who lives in St. Paul, Minnesota. She is deeply concerned about the status of workers in today's organizations.

Global Feminism

Merle Woo and Nancy Reiko Kato

Their new world order is everywhere and we detest it.

This imperialist community can only spell doom for the rest of us. But no amount of marketing can sell their ideas because we won't buy them. The majority of us belong to another class, a different race, the other sex, a different sexual orientation, a fresh generation, or an opposing world view.

Our lives and destinies are intertwined because of a common enemy—the international bankers, warmongers, and their government officials and police forces. What we share is the simple desire to work together to right the wrongs that seem to disproportionately hit women and people of color the hardest. Ours is a community of activists who live by the belief that "no one is free unless all of us are free" and that "an injury to one is an injury to all."

Only by building a community that moves toward confronting the powers that be will we be able to achieve our fullest human potential. As women, our life experiences provide us with the greatest potential to ensure that we will make it into the twenty-first century. We refuse to fight for one part of ourselves at the expense of the whole of our beings. We recognize inequality and censorship, and we won't tolerate it.

In the United States, we live in the belly of the beast. We must accept the responsibility of building the revolution here at home. The greatest act of solidarity that we can provide to our sisters and brothers internationally is to destroy the capitalist class that prevents them from completing their revolutions.

By uniting against the world's imperialists, we can pave the way for a society that provides for the basics. Soup kitchens, shantytowns, illiteracy, preventable diseases, and gang killings will be obsolete. Planning and production for the needs of people and not profits will determine what needs to be done. And those of us who have been previously disregarded because we are women, or people of color, or uneducated, or young, or old, old lesbian, will have equal voices in this new socialist society. We deserve nothing less.

The nineties is a tumultuous decade during which we are all being cast into the whirlwind of change. It is up to us to decide what kind of change we want and will work for.

The future is ours to determine. We look forward to it.

Merle Woo is an assistant professor at the University of California at Berkeley. Nancy Reiko Kato is a member of Radical Women.

Broke? Form a cooperative. Pool your resources money, skills, food and energy. Run day care centers for one another. It will save the lives of our children and allow us to work. Act like we are a tribe because dammit we are. Find an organization that gives you the skills needed to build your dream. Barter. Get out of the mainframe of a system which has decided to destroy you—create your own. Our ancestors and elders had their own ways, that is how we have survived to this day.

—Conversation with Cheryl Hawke, 1992

Believing in Ourselves

Carla Trujillo

The common boundary of "woman," per se, is often not enough to compensate for other areas of difference, particularly along the lines of race, class, and sexual preference. Each and every one of us is affected in some way by society's unjust views. Creating community means we must all make a continual effort to rid these poisons from our hearts and minds. Similarly, we must seek to dispel our insecurities about feeling that we need to be perfect with respect to the issues of racism, sexism, homophobia, and so on. Fear of making errors keeps us defensive, hostile, and unable to truly open up to one another.

I have accepted the fact that I am not a perfect person, but I am committed to unlearning old behaviors, prejudices, and unhealthy coping mechanisms. This process brings up a lot of fear that, I am sure, many of us can relate to. Recognizing our fears and talking about them to someone who cares about us enable us to work through them. This is growth and it's never easy.

I have also found that if I am vulnerable to others, they in turn are often vulnerable to me. Folks open up, listen, and learn. This can be scary, but I find that I have opened up my heart and the hearts of many others to positive growth.

When I am at my lowest ebb and filled with despair over our treatment of the world and one another, someone will surprise me and tell me that she is volunteering at a shelter for homeless teenagers, learning Spanish, or simply sitting with someone who is dying of cancer. When this happens, I sit for a minute and remember that we can still believe in ourselves and in our capacity for retaining our humanity. This, for me, is the ultimate in creating community.

Carla Trujillo is the editor of Chicana Lesbians: The Girls Our Mothers Warned Us About, *an administrator and lecturer at the University of California at Berkeley, and an editor with* Outlook *magazine.*

Misuigi Forssen

Art as Healing

Three Voices

Misuigi Forssen

In my work I try to see the extraordinary in the ordinary, to infuse magic and myth into our view of everyday life. We all tend to tell ourselves our own story, and in the telling try to glean the fact from the fiction. I am interested in having the fact and fiction collide to form a fabricated dialogue that in essence turns into a kind of truth. This truth, the things we all imagine to be true—our feelings, hopes, fears, and dreams—are very much a part of who we are.

The focus of my current work deals with the notion of a reconstructed or fictionalized personal history, coming from a racially mixed background—my mother is Korean, my father is American—has caused me to puzzle over my identity within this culture, the culture of my father. I was born in Korea and came to this country when I was four. Like many immigrants, my mother focused on learning and teaching me to be American at the expense of any Korean cultural education. Growing up in such a culturally diverse country as America can in some ways be quite homogenizing. I never really questioned my Korean origins because I never felt Korean, beyond the fact that I look Asian.

As time has gone on, these questions of personal identity, as well as a greater desire to explore and find a cultural identity, have surfaced in my work. My revitalized curiosity toward my Asian background caused me to ask my mother if I could look at pictures from the family albums. To my sadness she told me that my younger sister had taken all the photo albums and, through time and accident, had lost the majority of them. I was amazed at how empty I felt, as if I had no real past because the visual record had been destroyed. As time went on, I found myself drawn to looking at old portraits and tintypes from the turn of the century. These portraits of anonymous people began to be for me glimpses of personal histories similarly lost or abandoned. This brought me to wonder about constructing a personal past for myself. I discovered that I could take the few fragments that were left from the photo albums and create a fictional past that dealt more with my feelings about growing up and less with the actual events of it.

Through the process of my work I've tried to keep the humor and wonder of passage that I feel my life has been, as I feel all lives are. We are all very complex beings with a multitude of exposed and hidden aspects. Much of my work is about searching out the many layers of existence that make up the tapestry of our lives, to explore identity, to discover that the various differences people have with one another are actually what unite us to each other. We all are comprised of layers of experiences that shape how and who we are. Although we tend to feel quite singular, we are in fact quite multifaceted; we are layer upon layer upon layer.

Stephanie Johnson

Many of my pieces are homages to the ancestors. As an African American woman artist, I believe it is essential to create and re-create myself and my own images. I believe in synchronicity, karma, and racial memory. My work is about the survival and prosperity of people, specifically women, particularly women of African descent. I believe that I must elevate all my sisters in every aspect of my life and that failure to do so amounts to suicide.

My work focuses primarily on two visual elements: archival material (newspaper clippings, photos, advertisements) and projected light. Printed materials are salvaged from dusty archives and reconstructed by cutting, painting, and layering. The resulting slide montages are presented as projections in specific architectural settings (buildings facades, church interiors). The combination of projected light and architectural elements symbolizes the balance between the spiritual and material world, heaven and earth. Timelessness, a recurrent theme in my work, is conveyed by the ethereal nature of light. In my current installations, it is the repetition of form and materials that is meant to evoke remembrances in the viewer, and invoke ancestral spirits to the site of these memories.

Nadema Agard-Smith

As a visual artist with an indigenous perspective, I see art as a language of the spirit and a capsule of the culture. Indigenous art is a spiritual shorthand of color, design, and form of pigment to convey information to the subconscious or collective consciousness, which connects with a more profound understanding. "Art," in indigenous terms, is integrative, living, ceremonial, functional, historical, and educational. We make art, we are art.

Traditional designs and forms are a visual vocabulary that serve the community in much the same way dictionaries and encyclopedias serve western society. Traditional artists...are culture bearers. The persistence of non-western arts of the Americas is born out of a natural resistance that employs all forms of survival.

Stephanie Johnson

Misuigi Forssen was born in Korea and came to this country when she was four. She is a Boston-based collage and assemblage artist trained at the Massachusetts College of Art.

Stephanie Johnson is a Berkeley-based artist. She has a B.F.A. from Emerson College in Boston, Massachusetts and a M.A. from San Francisco State University. Additionally, she is a professional lighting designer/scenographer working nationally and internationally in theater and film.

Nadema Agard-Smith is Adjunct Professor of Visual Arts at Bemidji State University in Minnesota. She is the recipient of fellowships from the Smithsonian Institute, National Endowment of the Arts, and the Phelps Stokes Institute.

Cheng Imm Tan at office, 1992

Healing from Oppression

Cheng Imm Tan

We share some common experiences and patterns, but each of us also has our unique struggles and hurts that need to be fully worked on and cleansed. To reclaim our power means we must peel away the different layers of oppression, to clearly see and name what the oppression is and to formulate a liberation policy for ourselves, to develop allies, and to stay closely connected to other Asians and people of color.

Asian histories have not been calm. Among and between us, we have often had a history full of conflicts. We have warred against one another and mistreated each other. We have been pitted against each other and other communities of color. We need to work on getting close to each other and to resist attacking and criticizing one another. We need to work on reclaiming our inherent interconnectedness. Our liberation cannot be fully achieved unless we refuse to be used, or co-opted. Our liberation is connected to the liberation of all people of color, and all people.

What Allies Can Do

1. Because of oppression many of us have forgotten that we are inherently complete, intelligent, whole, beautiful, powerful human beings who are closely connected to every other human being. Remind us of who we are.

2. To support us means understanding how the oppression works. At every opportunity, work with us to dismantle the structures that maintain and uphold oppression.

3. Be aware of the pull to forget about us. It is important to contradict our invisibility and our sense of significance on every level. Make our issues important issues, even if there are few or no Asians in your midst.

4. Deep isolation and terror is the core of our oppression. We will have our defenses up but really want to come out. Our allies need to keep coming after us, to really get in with us.

5. Don't get impatient with us. Notice, acknowledge, and appreciate our hard work as well as who we are. If you do not first notice our work, we will be unable to believe and hear your appreciation of us as people. Remem-

ber: appreciation of who we are regardless of our accomplishment is an important contradiction for us.

6.   One of the most effective ways to cut through our isolation is to show us how much you really like us, love us, and above all, want us. Show us that you understand that we are important to you. Show yourself, share your life and struggles. Be real with us!

7.   Encourage us to keep doing what we do well, while reminding us that it is OK to have feelings and to show them. It will help us let go of our terror. Let us know that this will not be judged or criticized. Remind us that we will not lose your respect and loving for having difficulties.

8.   Once you have made up your mind to commit to us, and have earned our trust, *be there for us* when we call for help. For us to be able to call for help is a total contradiction to our isolation and rigid self-reliance.

9.   Remind us of our power. We often don't have a sense that life can really be changed. This internalized oppression is often seen in the way we attribute fortunes and misfortunes to fate or the law of karma.

10. Remind us also of our significance as well as the importance of our own liberation. We have a hard time remembering to work directly on our oppression as Asians and making our liberation primary.

11. When working with refugees and immigrants, help us work on the losses we have endured because of the war, and in coming to a new land. We will often resist because it feels too hard. Keep encouraging us to talk about our experiences, and listen with genuine interest.

12. Work on your own feelings about Asians or getting close to Asians, then welcome us fully for who we are. Encourage us to show our Asian selves. Don't let us hide or trivialize ourselves, our achievements, or our significance.

13. Interrupt any self-criticism that you see, and interrupt any criticism, distrust, or competition that you see among Asians. Remind us that we share a deep and natural closeness with other Asians, and work with us in this direction.

14. Encourage, support, and promote our leadership. Understand that we are not only leaders among Asians, but among all people.

15. Although as Asians we share some common experiences, it is important to understand the particular and unique experiences and struggles of each Asian group and figure out how to be allies to each person and group.

16. Start support groups of allies to Asians. Get close to us and work with us to figure out how to support our liberation.

Asian liberation is central to the liberation of all people. Asian liberation is not only about Asians reclaiming power and significance, but being in the forefront, working toward the liberation of all people. As Asians, we are, first and foremost, humans intimately connected to all other humans.

Rev. Cheng Imm Tan is associate minister at large and director of the Asian Women's Project sponsored by the Unitarian Universalist Urban Ministry.

Three generations—Maria Ramos, bottom right

Speak To Me

Maria Ramos

In 1970, when they called her a nigger lover, a communist, and a lesbian, I asked her why. "Because it's true," she mused, "at least the first two." By 1976 she was a lesbian too. But that was only the beginning.

I never understood why my mother looked so free when she said that their words were true. Later on in life, I learned to decode this unfamiliar language. "Nigger lover" was the word for a person confronting the layers of racism in U.S. society; "communist" was someone who did not structure their world around greed; and a "lesbian" was a woman who questioned the proprietary rights men apparently had over women and their bodies. It was the language of freedom I was beginning to understand. But that was only a beginning.

I had to learn my father's language too. He spoke Spanish. I did not. He wanted us to be Americans. No accent. The only phrase I knew in the language that was foreign to my tongue was *"Yo quiero agua,"* literally, "I want water." What I was really teaching myself to say was "I'm thirsty for the bloodline of my Cuban ancestry." My roots. The deep well of me and the tongue of history in my veins.

When my mother, the firstborn daughter of two Jewish parents, married my father in 1960 she was Catholic convert. So, naturally, I believed I was a Catholic. Luckily, my Spanish-speaking Catholic friends taught me to translate the language of the Catholic religion: Girls who had sex were "whores," "bad girls," and "sluts." The rules were very clear cut, easy to interpret. At school, I could point out the bad ones quickly because they were the wild ones—the ones who had an unfettered, unharnessed anger and attitude. I learned to disdain those girls and learned how to feel good about not feeling good about others—one of the first tenets of so many world religions.

The Catholic language taught me that my sexuality was bad and dangerous, too, because I could get pregnant. I was twenty-one years old before I had sex. I was glad to have remained pure for so long a time. It made me better than the rest. For a very long time I believed that was all I had to show for who I was: a "good girl." When I went outside the morning after having intercourse for the first time, I truly believed people would know that my market value had fallen steeply. I wondered what I would do with myself now that I was not special anymore. I believed this for a long time too.

But what about my Jewish heritage? A dialect that haunted. The language of denial was spoken to me as well. Bodies of flesh dropped onto bodies of flesh, and I heard someone say it didn't happen. So maybe when you talk to me, don't tell me I don't look Jewish, OK? Or if you must say it, don't say it as if it were a compliment.

When you speak to me of affirmative action, make sure we speak the same language. Don't think that I don't know you think it's only because of my Spanish last name that I went to an Ivy League school. Yes, my education has given me the key to understanding that exposing myself to what would otherwise have been an all-white, upper-class environment made them all better. They have touched me and seen life from the mind of a woman who is a Cuban Catholic Jew raised by a lesbian niggerloving communist who served food to people who could afford the luxury of eating out in restaurants so she could afford the luxury of feeding her three kids. I was a prepackaged cultural experience for my classmates, but now I speak the language of the institution, too.

Sometimes people tell me that they want to have more "minorities" in their organizations/clubs/schools and on their faculties/committees/boards, but they can't find them. I want to speak the sarcastic language I know so well and say, "Have you tried looking under a rock?—that is normally where we hide." But sometimes I cannot speak, sometimes I cannot find that voice inside me, or any voice. Sometimes I don't know what to say, even after all the languages I've learned.

And I know how to speak something else. I learned the first word the day I saw my best friend slapped hard in the face by her boyfriend. I learned the unspoken language of power. Sometimes I think that that's the language we all speak best. It may very well be the official language of the United States of America. It's spoken in the corporate boardroom and in the hallway of the apartment in the ghetto. It's spoken by the husband to the wife and to his girlfriend and to the prostitute and to a female co-worker all in the same breath. Bad breath. It's spoken by the mother to her children and by the manager at McDonald's to his serfs, by the master to his slave, and by the bully to the person holding onto fear. It's spoken by gangs. It's spoken by lovers and politicians to one another in the bedroom of Congress. Junkies speak it and smack speaks it and crack talks it too.

When my best friend didn't speak back to him, I did, and they called me a lesbian. (Now things were starting to sound familiar, for this was a language I already knew.) Several years later, she married him. Every morning he would lock her inside the apartment and take the phone cord with him. She didn't know that she could speak back. She was absent the day they taught us that in school. I was absent that day, too. Did they teach us that in school?

But I learned how to speak back to power from my mother. In 1976 she opened our home as a shelter for battered women and their children. Everyone wanted to know why she never locked the front door to our house—wasn't she scared that the batterers would come looking for "their" wives or girlfriends?

"They get their power from fear," she would respond calmly, "There is no fear here. They have no power."

Now I can also speak back.

My languages are many, and I spend endless days and nights in dreams, trying to talk to you. Hear all that I have to say; listen to my voices and try to understand. Don't tell me I'm hard to get to know. Are you listening? Can you hear me? Don't ask me how I am and not really care. Listen. Don't assume we speak the same language. Listen. So you can Hear.

Maria Ramos was born in Hackensack, New Jersey; she moved to California in 1980 to attend the University of California at Berkeley where she majored in criminal justice. She attended the University of Pennsylvania School of Law and currently teaches criminal law, legal ethics & domestic relations at New College School of Law in San Francisco.

Ehulani Kane

Ancestral Healing

Interview with Ehulani Kane

Interviewed in my kitchen July 1993, Ehulani sat sipping tea and looking for all the world like a cousin of mine. She speaks softly, slowly; the way she says "all" or "belong" sometimes becomes a song. Laughing, she said, "I have a love affair with my name, Ehulani Hope Kane. Ehu? When Hawaiian children are born and they are more light-skinned or have red in their hair, they are called Ehu-children. Lani means heaven. And my father's family name was Kane which means man. My father died when I was a young child. That is something on my altar to do, to find that part of my family. Anyway, it makes sense to claim Kane as my name because I was given my father's name at birth and there was that male part of my consciousness that needed to be brought forward. I work towards bringing that male and female in balance. All four of my children have Hawaiian names. They move in the world with ease; that is something that comes from being Hawaiian." Listening to the boisterous joy of neighborhood children at play next door, we shared a remarkable two hours, portions of which I now share with you.
—E. F.

My mother was the eldest of sixteen children. My grandmother met my grandfather when she was a very young woman, maybe thirteen or fourteen. I am not quite sure of her age, but he had a couple of children already, and he was married. Then they fell in love, and my mother was the eldest of their coming together. He ended up marrying my grandmother, and they had eight children with each other. There were four boys and four girls. My grandfather's name was Joseph, and all the boys were named Joseph and all the girls were named Josephine. Everybody had his name.

My grandmother knew he was involved with selling alcohol illegally, but she didn't know he was also involved in gambling and prostitution. He was part of what today would be considered the Hawaiian Mafia. So, for Hawaiians at that time, they lived very well. Even then, because of so many people coming into the Hawaiian Islands the Hawaiians were very much second-class citizens.

My grandfather treated my grandmother really well, and I feel he protected her from this information. But when my mother was about eleven or twelve years old, his "business associates" tried to do away with him. They set the house on fire; nobody was at home except my grandfather. He didn't die immediately, but was severely burned and died three or four months later. My grandmother was pregnant and had her eighth child after he was dead. Later, I don't know how many years, she met her second husband.

He was very different than her first husband. I mean, he didn't work. When they married he wanted her to get rid of her children, to put them in foster care or send them off somewhere because they were not of his blood. He was very abusive to my mother and her siblings. And he was abusive to my grandmother also. My mother was the eldest and she hated him. She told me that when another baby was born, she would just cry and cry because it meant another baby to take care of.

By the time Mommy was sixteen, she married so she could get out of their house and take a lot of her brothers and sisters with her. So she continued to caretake. When she was eighteen or so she had my oldest sister, and by that time she was done with her husband. She left him because her siblings were old enough to take care of themselves. The ironic thing is that she let my grandmother raise my elder sister. She had hated that abusive home, yet she put her own daughter in that situation. But Mommy needed to live her life. So my sister was raised with my grandmother amongst many, many children.

My mother lived as she saw fit. Mommy was very spunky. She, for the most part, lived in Hawaii, but she came to the mainland and it was in that time that she met my father. One thing I remember my mother telling me is that she would never date Hawaiian men, because it was a negative to be Hawaiian, to be Hawaiian in our own land. *But* she met a Hawaiian man in San Francisco where she was working, while living with one of my uncles. I think they went off to Reno and got married. She soon realized she was pregnant. A few months later she realized that she didn't want to be married. So, before I was born, she was done with my father.

I was born in San Francisco. When I was five months old, my older sister, who was seventeen, flew over and brought me back home. My sister thought, though she was still living with my grandmother, I was going to be her baby.

But there were other things brewing. My grandmother and my sister lived way out in Laie, a Mormon community; they were Mormon. What the hell would you be Hawaiian and be a Mormon for? But it is a way to survive. "Let's adopt these totally white cultural values and go for it." The only sense I can maybe make of this choice is that the Mormons, like the

Hawaiians, are strong on family. I don't know.

Anyway, Honolulu was about fifty miles away from where they lived. It was decided that an auntie of mine would raise me, and not my sister. My sister was very upset; but she was only seventeen and had no say in the matter. For the first year and a half of my life, I was with my auntie, and my sister would come and see me. Then my mother came back from the mainland. She was newly married and pregnant with my little brother. She had married a man who was Portuguese, as was my sister's father. My brother is about two years younger than me. After he was born, we all lived together. There are four children, and I was the only one who had a Hawaiian father. My brother's father was also abusive; he was an amateur prizefighter or something like that. He had the same thing about me as my second grandfather had about my mother and her brothers and sisters. I wasn't his blood.

When I was about three years old some *haole* friends of my mother that she'd met while living in San Francisco, came to the Hawaiian islands. They were looking to adopt a child. They were going to adopt two cousins of mine who lived with my grandmother. Instead they hooked up with my mom, who was in a tricky situation, and the long and short of it is that she let me go back to the mainland with them.

As with so many native cultures, it is not that big a deal that, if you don't feel that you can raise your child, somebody within the family will raise the baby. The gesture was not unusual, but the fact that she allowed me to go out of the family and to go such a great distance, I found out years later, was really upsetting to everybody, especially my grandmother, the matriarch of the family. Over the next year or two, the people that became my adoptive parents needed to legally adopt me; to make sure that they had "ownership," you know. The reason that I mention all of this is because I was raised in Monterey; I was not raised at home.

My adoptive parents were older people. My adoptive father, Ed, was sixty-five when I was three. Jean was younger, in her late forties, early fifties, and it was the fifth marriage for each of them. Jean's background was Irish and English, or something. Ed's background was English American. Jean had never been able to have children because when she was fifteen, she had had difficulty with her bleeding. It wouldn't stop. So the way the doctors dealt with the problem was to do a hysterectomy. I believe that Jean was really crazy, in addition to alcoholism being their disease. So there was abuse as I was growing up—abusing alcohol and abusing me. But I think one of the deepest wounds came when they brought me home. It was really important for Jean to let people know that she had brought home a child from Hawaii. "Oh we have this little *Hawaiian* girl." It was important for her to let people know that I was not Negro.

They were racist. Jean was very racist. My features, my physical features…she would have me pinch my nose because my nose is flat. She had me do lip exercises because my lips are full, so they wouldn't stick out. Although to everybody on the outside it was "Oh this is my little Hawaiian doll," at home there were constant threats to send me back if I did not behave as they wanted me to, though home was a bad place and they had somehow saved me from it. My mother's lifestyle was really colorful—over the years she divorced my brother's father and was with quite a few other men. She had my little sister at forty-eight or forty-nine. The picture they presented of her was that she was a tramp, that she wasn't good. They had some distant respect for my grandmother. When I say "they," I really mean Jean because she was the more powerful of the two.

When I was younger, between three and five, they returned to Hawaii a few times to make the adoption legal. In California, Ed was too old to adopt a child, but Hawaii was not yet a state, so they did all the legal preceedings there. I remember that when I would go back home, even when I was little, I didn't feel like I belonged. I was being raised white. I couldn't talk local anymore… It was hard. In so many ways, I would say that it is not until the last ten years that I've truly been able to be in my body as a Hawaiian woman. And I can also say that the spirits of my ancestors have saved my life.

Ed was so old and had given over his power to Jean entirely, it was like he was not there. He was a real good person, but he gave it all away. Jean was the classic husband-beater. One time she actually hit him over the head with a rolling pin. I remember one evening after a scuffle when she had been physically violent. The next day he was taking me to school—I was probably about fourteen years old—and he said to me, "Well you know, Lani, I can't…you know, your mother doesn't really mean what she says. She really doesn't mean to do those things, but you know I can't say anything or she will hit me." When I think about him, I am baffled that someone could just give up their power so completely.

The deepest wound, which I still struggle with, is where do I belong? Because I didn't fit in. Though Jean did her best to try to make me be white. I wasn't white. Inside my voice would say, "I am not white…I am not white…" They put me in an all-girls Catholic school, which was yet another strange orientation. For some reason Mommy had baptized me Catholic; I don't know why. Maybe it was just rebellion—she didn't want to be Mormon like everybody else. So, in an effort to make sure that I would have my Catholic education—my adoptive parents were Protestants and not practicing church people at all—they put me in a very affluent Catholic school. This was a nice gesture on their part I think. I was there for twelve years, so all the Catholic stuff came in, too. It was a private, high falutin school, and after a certain point they couldn't afford it. They were really working-class people. Ed had been an electrician all his life, then bought some property, so he was comfortable financially. But that kind of school was too expensive after a while; so the nuns put me on scholarship.

Jean, Ed, and the nuns raised me to be white, and I wasn't white. And they raised me around really wealthy people. I was in this school where there was a class thing; I was in a class of people that I would not have ever been in. It was an opportunity on a certain level, but we're talking people like Hearsts and Bechtels, people like that. I was one of one or two people of color throughout my twelve years of education. So there was always this strangeness of not belonging.

When I was little my grandmother had such an impact on me. I don't know why. Grandmother was a beautiful woman: probably about three hundred pounds—very little, but very big; this beautiful face, grey hair; and just her *mana*, her spirit, was so big you couldn't help but feel it. Maybe she was praying for my life the whole time. I don't know. But she died when I was nine years old. We—Jean and Ed and I—visited Hawaii when I was nine years old, and it was the last time I saw her. She made a luau for me; I couldn't figure out why. Every time I went home there was such a struggle inside of me. There was part of me that didn't trust my mother, so I would always kind of go toward my older sister. I think I technically bonded with her more as an infant than with my mother. I felt safer as a child and as a young adult hanging with my sister, and I was getting all this junk information about my mother—"she is bad," all this stuff. You know.

When this luau was given for me, I felt kind of stupid. Not the center of attention or anything, just that this luau is for Lani. I remember that I would just watch my grandmother—she was such a mystery to me. Shortly after that visit she passed on. And I remember I would pray to her, that's who I would pray to. I mean everything was taken away from me—language was taken away from me, culture was taken away from me. I would pray to my grandmother.

Over the years as I talked with my mother about my life, listening beyond her excuses, one of the things I heard and believed was that giving her child to *haole* people was one of the greatest gifts she could have given. And though over the years it was evident to her that I was being mistreated, there was nothing she could do about it. Legally I belonged to them. In the beginning my mother would send me money, would send me things on my birthday, but after awhile Jean said no more contact with my family. By the time I was eighteen, "my parents" and my mother were not good friends anymore. That's ironic.

One other irony: I believe one reason my mother let me go was because Ed and Jean were comfortable, and she wanted a good life for me. When I was about ten years old, daughters from Ed's previous marriage, who were almost the same age as Jean, stripped him of the property he had continued to hold jointly and amicably with his ex-wife since their marriage. Though divorced, they had remained business partners. There had been no hassle. When the first wife died, their daughters, due to some resentment, took the property somehow. I believe it had to do with his age and taking his power of attorney. By this time his income was solely from his property because he didn't work anymore, and the daughters took it away. That meant Jean had to get a job. She worked in a convalescent home until her death.

At this same time, though my mother never lived high on the hog, she was doing pretty well. She had a bar in Kona. She was doing fine, man, she was doing fine. So the reason she had let me go didn't wash, in terms of how fate played things out. But her love never went away from me, you know. Up until she died I would call her on my birthday every year and thank her for my life. She had let me come through.

My struggles, my original wound caused have been psychological trauma. It's been about identity—in my twenties and early thirties it was about "Who am I?" and "Where do I belong?" OK. It was very psychological. A lot of depression, a lot of going repetitively into dark places inside myself. I don't think I ever did deep abuse to myself, but the emotional situations I would get into were abusive in many ways.

So that when we talk about Healing, I would say again, all through these years of my life I feel like my spirits, my ancestors have taken care of me. I would say that within the last eight to ten years of my life, the thing that's finally been able to kick in is that the healing comes from the fact that I *am* Hawaiian. I have chosen these "garments" of my cultural identity for this lifetime for good reason. Claiming myself and my identity as a Hawaiian person is what will continue to allow me to heal all these wounds. It is what saved my life all the way along.

People hear the complex events of my childhood and say, "Man, you're really strong." But it is my consciousness, my strength comes from the cellular memory of my people. The graciousness of my culture has allowed me to get through everything, thus far. It was a real fucking drag to have gone through all the things I've gone through. I feel hurt, really hurt. But Mommy did the best she could for me, or what she thought was best at the time. I am not mad at her.

The *mana*, spirit, of my grandmother was a presence so steady and strong you couldn't help but feel it. My mother had it too, especially as she got older. After the death of my grandmother, Mommy was the matriarch, and we have a huge family. One of the qualities of being Hawaiian that is really essential and important is listening. That is how you learn. I think that the *haoles* don't understand about that. They can be intellectual, putting things in place, really smart, but…there is a native intelligence—you watch and you listen, there was that about my grandmother. You walked into the room, and you could feel her energy. She also had tremendous love, tremendous *aloha*. To be Hawaiian is to have the *aloha* spirit. The *aloha* spirit is much more than the little ditties in the advertisements. It is a way of life.

I can get way political with you in terms of the Hawaiian sovereignty struggle. I think it is important the righteous way many people in our Hawaiian community are finally speaking up, the anger that's coming through is very appropriate. The thing about the Hawaiians is that the *aloha* spirit is what holds everything. There is a way that people might disagree and say that Hawaiians have to be brave and strong and courageous to get our rights, and that is also true. We can be that way, yet love is still what holds it all. Being Hawaiian means living with *aloha* in all we do.

I was supposed to live in two worlds, you know. It was part of my destiny. And there is a way that I'm never going to be as local as I want to be when I go home to Hawaii, because that wasn't in the plan. But Hawaii is my home, Hawaii is my family, Hawaii is my lifeline. My grandmother is my guardian angel, and my mother is the source from which I came. I pray to them and to my father and grandfather. It feels important to do that now. Because the males were missing when I was growing up, it's their turn to be here for me in the best and most important spirit ways when I need help.

So I continue to live in two cultures. But as I grow older I realize I am a Hawaiian girl. That is why I do things the way that I do. I remember Mommy used to say out loud to me, "You are Hawaiian you know. You are Hawaiian." It didn't make any sense because I felt I didn't belong, like I wasn't Hawaiian because I wasn't with my family. And she would say that to me over and over again. I didn't know what that meant because so much was taken away. Now I know. I just have to keep making spiritual notations, keeping track of where I am emotionally and spiritually.

All I can do is *be* who I am and pass on the essentials of what is important in terms of being a human being, in terms of being Hawaiian about living with *pono* (truth) and *aloha*. Sometimes that is really hard for me. It feels like a compromise and I know it's not. As long as I don't compromise my heart and my spirit anymore. I remember my ancestors...with them I walk life in righteousness and beauty.

Ehulani Kane was born in 1955 under an Aries sun, the goddess Pele, representing the strong and silent glow guiding her through this lifetime. She is a singer, dancer, writer, teacher, producer, and director constantly trying to find TRUTH, BEAUTY, and HUMOR in being a single mother of four children, ages sixteen, thirteen, eleven and nine, in a society that doesn't fully honor the value of the mother or the artist.

We Black Lesbians carry some level of self-loathing that may never leave us unless we undertake some serious self-examination and honest sharing... It is important that we begin to really listen to how we speak of and refer to other Black Sisters, how we critically judge by color before we give ourselves the precious chance to learn what miracles we all are. We must cease addressing our skins first as others outside our culture do, and strive toward self-understanding and self-love. This can be quickly gained if we only take a step toward that goal on our own.

— Terri L. Jewell, "A Call to Black Lesbian Sisters"

Luisah Teish

Multi-Colored Momas

Interview with Luisah Teish

With Teish and me things rarely go according to plan; the day we were to do this interview was no exception. We shopped in Berkeley and Oakland for last-minute items she needed for an upcoming trip to Spain. As the hours passed, I learned a marvelous chant to Queen Asphalta, the goddess of parking, and had moments of intense discomfort because Teish's information about the relationship between my daughter and me set me thinking about my brother, now five years dead. I felt transparent and vulnerable for some minutes, then decided that we could work with this newly revealed hurt on another day. Returning to her home, we sat in an ancestral hut consecrated to a spirit-guide named Frieda, eating pastries and fruit as we talked about freedom and laughed, ate and laughed some more. Here are portions of our sisterly discussion that golden day in June.
—E. F.

There is a chant something to the effect of "White cowry shells against the black buttocks, those who have seen the rump of Oschun have seen the beauty of the world." Compare that to all these descriptions we have of the love goddess in Cuba and in Haiti. There she is always a fair-skinned mulatto with long hair. This speaks profoundly to the effect of colonization. The standard of beauty has changed from the dark-skinned woman who is like the Queen of the Forest, the natural daughter of her environment, to this Miss Anne woman, a luxurious white woman or a luxurious mulatto whose standard of beauty depends upon her standing on the backs of somebody else. Her household and her luxury exists because a dark-skinned woman is out in the field, enslaved. We have a lot to learn from how we women of color have taken a political and economic imbalance and internalized it. The big mistake is accepting that standard of beauty. I understand it coming from the colonizer, but when we internalize and start to believe it, then we have a real problem.

One of the things I think about is our childhood rhymes. You know, "The blacker the berry the sweeter the juice, when it comes to your color it just ain't no use." I also think about how in so many Black families—like mine—we have a bouquet of roses. I have cousins who are what you call in Louisiana, *passe bon*, so fair you can see the blue veins in their skin. They could pass for white. Some do when it is necessary. We run a wide spectrum, all the way to telephone black like my brother. Some of us are blue-black, with me running the red-brown in between.

They say down South if a woman was yellow, a "yella hammer," her features didn't have to be that fine. If they were, that was a nice addition, but that yellow skin was enough to have people invest the hope that if a fair-skinned man—another Creole man—married this quadroon, they would produce children who would have a better life because of their lighter skin color. That is categorically *not* real. Once in a while it has brought economic advantage, but in terms of the person's individual life, that has not held true.

On the other hand, when I was growing up, when a black-skinned girl was beautiful, she was exceptionally beautiful. She was dark, dark, dark with sparkling eyes and brilliant teeth, and usually with long hair and great muscles, and she had to have a powerful presence. She was looked upon as a gift from the ancestors, a walking example of our power to sustain ourselves in spite of all. I was always in the middle range, looking at the two sides.

That really crystallized for me as an adult while I lived in the Northwest. I was placed in a situation where I had two roommates—one high-yellow with red hair, and the other coal black with deep brown eyes. And, again, there I was, the one in the middle. It taught me a lot, watching us go through our changes, watching us deal with the blessing and the curse of the standards attributed to our skin shades. For example—I'm talking the late sixties now—you had a phenomenon in the midst of the so-called revolution, when black was supposed to be beautiful, where a fair-skinned sister with a natural was the best of both worlds to some brothers. He could get an almost-white woman with Black consciousness and could fulfill that other fantasy without the guilt, you see.

What I heard from the light-skinned sister often was: "If he really wants a white woman, why don't he go get one, instead of messing with me? Because I'm really trying to be black." At the same time, in a situation where she wanted something, she knew if the competition were darker-skinned sisters, she had an extra feather in her cap because she was fair. If we were lined up to be chosen, then she had an extra puppy chip. Do you know what I mean by a puppy chip? You know, the things that make you cute.

The dark-skinned sister that I lived with was pursued most by young white men—ironic at that time of great cultural identity. A lot of brothers were into white women, not so much as an act of affection, but as a political act. The counterpoint to that was a few bold white men who were looking to discover, well, "What is this secret about blackness?" I guess their logic was: if I'm going to do this, let me really do it and really look at somebody *black*. So, I watched this sister going through her changes, not necessarily being approached by brothers, but feeling like she might be betraying the race by dating white men. And at the same time, back then, we were exploring new relationships and shifting stuff around sort of frantically, not wanting to mimic what had occurred in the fifties, but not knowing exactly where to go. There was a hippie movement going on, and I watched what I used to call the Count of Monte Cristo syndrome, where you'd see white people one day and they would be dressed as Jesus, Mary, and Joseph. The next day they'd be the Three Musketeers. People were trying to act out new identities, and Black Americans did not escape that.

Interestingly enough, being the middle color, I found myself in a very satisfactory position. In terms of dressing I could wear any color—I could wear anything. Pale sisters couldn't wear certain things, and a dark sister knew that if she wore a red dress it would create a scandal. I could put on anything. And in that whole push-pull between who is attracted to whom, I could basically attract any kind of man I wanted because I was some kind of safe middle ground.

In a lot of ways, I think being born in family where there were a number of shades, and especially being born in the South, prepared me for dealing with all of this. What was always hard for me was getting full acceptance for what my skin color represented. I've taken family and ancestry seriously for a long time. With my mother's mother being Native American and her father being Black, one of the hardest things for me was, in the fifties, if I mentioned my mother's mother, some white person would tell me to be quiet about that because if there was anything worse than being a "nigger," it was being an "Indian." OK? Then in the sixties, if I said anything about my mother's mother, somebody would accuse me of trying to not be Black. And so, you kind of got to this place where you didn't say anything and let everybody think that you were whatever they needed to think you were.

In the meantime, of course, there is looking strongly at one's African identity and trying to find out who my people are—and getting three distinct answers. Africans from West Africa would look at me and immediately say, "Dahomey woman," usually prefaced with "uppity." East Africans, especially during my bald period—I was bald for four or five years—would swear I was Masai. I don't look Masai to me, but they would identify with the hairdo. Other people would say, yes, you look like your people are from the Congo. Well, Dahomey and Congo make sense. In terms of my real ancestry, I know it was Ewe and Congo.

I usually think of myself as good strong stock, but when I went to Senegal and Nigeria for the first time, I encountered women who were so beautifully black that I remember having a day I actually felt weak and washed out because the Senegalese women are startlingly beautiful—in their personal carriage, in their dress, the way they sing, in the way they move. And where dark-skinned Sisters here were taught for a long time that success means wearing muted colors, unh-unh, they play that thing to the hilt in Senegal. The telephone-black sister will throw on some red and some gold, with a burst of brilliant cobalt blue. And you just go, "OK, girl, wear it out!" Ultimately what it did was reinforce my tendency to say I don't follow fashion, I set it. I will set it around my ethnicity and around what feels good to me.

We need to be aware of what different skin tone meant politically and economically in a historical context. But at this time in our evolution as a species, and especially at this point in the women's movement, women of color having issues with each other over color is redundant. The whole world has issue with us over color—why should we have issue among ourselves? Its really like a minstrel show, doing an imitation of an imitation of yourself. I would like to offer the notion of a bouquet of flowers. If we thought of ourselves as a bouquet of flowers with rich blues and deep reds, brilliant yellows, sparkling greens, if we could see ourselves as a bouquet rather than as colors that need to stand against each other, or that are better than the others, or blending into just one shade—such foolishness—if we could really think culturally in that way, I believe we'd add more richness to our culture.

That process may have to begin simply with honestly telling each other our stories and saying what having various tones has meant to us and has done to us and how people have reacted to us.

I hope this book will open up some loving dialog, and entice us to create some stories and some material that will stop the next generation from going through this. I see it already. I see it happening one more time already, and it really shouldn't. Really, it shouldn't.

I want to take the opportunity to say, especially to fair-skinned sisters, that they should not assume fair skin means European ancestry. Africa is a continent, and She is the Mother of *all* humanity. We should not be shocked to find examples of all the children somewhere in Her belly. We are a bouquet of roses on the Continent, and we were a bouquet of roses on the Continent before the European invasions, because what we know as the "European" evolved from us. So, I would like to take the opportunity to snatch away from those sisters, both the privilege and the burden of imagined difference that they may be entertaining. When a person does have European ancestry or Native [American] ancestry or whatever, if it was acquired honorably especially, it serves one to get to know something about that, so you understand what is running around in your genes. Whatever shade you are, whatever race you are, you always want to know enough about yourself so that you can stand in the presence of other humans as equals.

When people go sliding in there thinking, well, I'm a rape baby, or I'm just the descendant of a slave, or I'm a mule because I'm yellow, or I'm better because I'm yellow, or I'm less because I'm black, or I'm strange because I'm orange, or I'm weird because I'm brown, or I'm funny because I'm red—you've got to get rid of all of that and take a look at the grand design of nature. Nature loves color. Green is one of her favorites, not black or white, but green and then blue. Then the yellow-orange of the sun. We have to start looking at it in that way.

I remember one time I made a doll for my Oschun, and I used black fabric and yellow yarn for the doll's hair. Somebody leaped all over me and said. "What are you doing making Oschun a blond." I said, "Excuse me, do you think white women own the color yellow?" I am Mother Africa; everything that's on this planet I owned first, including the color yellow. We have to keep that kind of thing in perspective; otherwise it will destroy us.

The thing that will save us is the realization that we have license to be a rainbow; we have all of nature to choose from in decorating ourselves. I am very vain about being a Black woman. I am. That's why I want to read multi-colored Moma to you. Back in 1975 I was doing some mental-patient advocacy work in San Francisco. I got hooked up with this sister, a prominent psychologist. We were doing fine until she came to visit my house.

I am a kind of frustrated visual artist, you know, so I draw things and stick them up on the wall. I had done this thing I called a self-portrait, very cubist. (I am not going to say "Picasso-esque," because he got it from us.) She came in, looked, and said, "I see. You have a very heavy fantasy life, don't you?" And in the moment she said that, it did something to me. I felt myself shrink. I felt myself close up. I felt the need to cover myself. It happened physically. And when she left, I said, "I can't let this be this way." As a result of that experience I wrote "The Vanity Series." I said I would write a series of poems that would take all the things people would have me be ashamed of, and I would brag about them. This poem is from that series.

Vanity Series One Multi-Colored Moma

> My sweet coffee skin
> holds secrets in its shade,
> whispers silent warnings
> to a black and white world.

Do not box me
  in your narrow racial jackets
    too tight to move in,
      too thin to wear.

My brown pores bleed
  with the sweat of many nations,
    generations of colors
      ooze down my arm.

My Bantu behind
  plays the drums of dancing griots,
    telling stories with my sway
      singing songs with each step

My high Choctaw cheekbones
  love the Mississippi Delta.
    Remember Running Cloud's daughter
    and the Red Man gone.

My breasts angle 'round,
  like the dark gypsy wenches.
    Crescent moons touch my belly.
    Silver slithers on my throat.

My almond eyes sparkle
  to the sound of Eastern jingles.
    Glass chimes dress my eyelids.
    Tinkling bells kiss my brow.

My dirty red hair
  speaks of crazy Cajun cousins,
    talks of fair Creole ladies
      and their dark Spanish men.

My Tibetan thighs open
  and the Red Sea splits.
    My soft lips part
      between Dahomey and Brazil.

My sweet coffee skin
   holds secrets in its shade.
   Whispers silent warnings
      to a black and white world.

I will not wear
   your narrow racial jackets
      as the blood of many nations
      run sweetly thru my veins

And that's the way I feel about it.

I can remember a point in my life when I made a clear decision that I would not do the kind of kowtowing to yellow-skinned Sisters that I had seen other darker-skinned Sisters do. I realized that certain yellow-skinned women expected to be catered to, expected that people would fall all over them. They believed in what they thought was skin-color privilege. When I peeped it, I said, "OK, I am going to erase that. I will respond to that Sister based on her personality, not that [color] thing there. And not in a predetermined way." Because the flip side of kowtowing is that sometimes, in the middle of trouble, that yellow-skinned sister can become a target. Everybody decides to hate her as the personification of the injustice. I made a clear commitment to myself that I will treat her like anybody else.

Traveling around the world there is this illness that has been left everywhere. You can go to New Zealand and you will find it—this issue about light and dark; you go to India and you find it. On this point, as on all others, I want to invoke the dormant cells in the human brain to wake up and show us another way to BE. Because to waste precious time and energy on such as that, instead of enjoying the bouquet, is one of the few things that I think is a sin. I hope that something in this interview touches that yellow Sister, that brown Sister, that red Sister, that Black Sister in a way that will make her lift her chin and stick her chest out and say: I am beautiful just as I am, because you are. And the Goddess loves you all.

Dr. Luisah Teish, born and raised in New Orleans, is a priestess of Oshun in the Yoruba Lucumi tradition. She is a dancer, choreographer, storyteller, actress, teacher, activist, feminist, and writer. Her book Jambalaya *(published by Harper & Row) is a sacred collection of personal charms and practical rituals.*

Vanessa May

One Sister's Love of Beauty

Vanessa May

Personally, I ill fit into this society and I am very glad that is so. This is a society on a collision course with itself. And as the spread of these societal values moves across the globe in the name of a "New World" order, we place ourselves on the brink of destruction.

—V. May

Beautiful smiles on beautiful faces, each one's roots from different places, but all finding asylum on the lunch benches of Brainard Avenue's elementary school.

Beautiful, wondrous world sisters whose cultures spanned the globe. Latin America, Europe, Asia, and Africa. Susan Rico. Mindy Nakamura. Barbara Rivers. Tracy Sketerman. Lisa Belson. Vanessa May.

Sisters of Gaea, daughters of Eve, all finding a common ground on which to stand and to communicate. Enjoying each other's company and appreciating our differences.

That is, until the fifth grade, when the joys of childhood became the pangs of prepubescence. One's racial, cultural, sexual, and social identities were questioned. Are you Black? Are you trying to be white? Are you fruity? Are you cool? Are you? What are you?

It was during this time that societal constructs laid siege to free hearts, minds, and souls. White girls do not hang out with Black girls unless they want to be Black. Asian girls don't hang out with Mexicans unless they wanna be Mexican. Girls must like boys unless they are weird, and you must have certain clothes to define you and the group to which you belong. Conform or rebel. Something that all preteens and teens do, to a greater or lesser degree.

Our society sets into motion divide-and-conquer tactics that rip at the very essence of our being. To question societal constructs is to live a life of one's own making, and how many of us can create for ourselves a mode of behavior that will allow for existence in a society that by design systematically destroys deviance?

Moreover, people are taught that in order to be truly socialized one must act in a manner that doesn't deviate far from Puritanical European roots. Prosperous roots that built one of the mightiest nations the world has ever known. A nation whose reputation is based on exported lies and untruths. A nation that holds all other nations captive. Nations, striving to be like her, engage in a process that is destroying the world.

How?

First: indoctrinate people with the inane idea that white is powerful. It appears to be so. Modern history shows us white world domination. The subjugation of people of color worldwide gives an appearance of power—not the reality of a paranoid humanoid whose fear of extinction causes it to destroy all that seems to threaten it.

Second: indoctrinate people with the insane idea that the way in which they have lived for thousands of years is wrong, "primitive." Compare a grass hut to a skyscraper. Compare hunting and gathering food every day with going to the refrigerator or McDonald's. Don't discuss the reality of ecologically unsound structures that recycle stale air, spread disease, and create waste in such amounts that we can't dispose of it. Ignore the reality that hunting and gathering places in perspective—the value of life and death, need and want, animals, plants, and humans and our interdependence.

In conclusion: create a zero-sum social construct that teaches superiority based on innate inferiority and teach *all* people to aspire to it. In their aspiration they continually lose but appear to gain. The model appears to continually gain power, wealth, position, and value; all the while it wreaks havoc in order to keep up appearances. In reality we all lose.

Societal constructs lay siege to young, impressionable minds, hearts, and souls. Taught not to appreciate our distinct and unique cultures, we are taught instead to treat them with mistrust and suspicion. Sell out. Renounce your family's ways, adopt a prepackaged societal identity. You must fit into one of them but it cannot, it *must* not, be based on your own culture or on an eclectic multicultural view. It must be based on white supremacy, based of the idea that you and other people of color are inferior. Not just your looks, but your actions. You cannot be civil toward each other because in your quest to be like white, you must all fight for its favor.

Can we cease to care about how we are seen in the eyes of our lighter kin? Can we see ourselves with our own eyes? Can we find the beauty in ourselves? Can we see with wisdom, the eternal wisdom each young child has that assures that we all are one? A wisdom that lets the soul see, the heart act, and the mind think.

I love beauty. Beauty to me comes in all shades, shapes, and sizes. I must see life this way. I can also see ugliness. It too comes in all shades, shapes, and sizes. What differentiates beauty from what is ugly is behavior.

Western society directs people to see beauty with only one vision. (Note the *Miss Universe Pageant*: The majority of the world's people are people of color, yet the majority of the contestants of the pageant are white-skinned.)

I let my mind open and the ideas came forth. I cannot help my love of beauty. I cannot quell my love of life. I cannot be blinded, nor let others define my visions. I know what I see.

Sisterfriends, you all are very beautiful! Now, I know I've never seen you, but Beauty can be felt as well as seen; and I feel your beauty.

My definition of beauty is not based on any European standard or any European mind-set. If it were, I would hate myself, and probably hate or envy you. I've come to understand that beauty truly is in the eye and soul of the beholder. Understanding this has made me an extremely happy woman. I take sheer delight in appreciating my fellow human beings and in appreciating all that this world and life has to offer.

Women of color, particularly African American women, have been debased and devalued based on their hue. For "some strange reason," the lighter hued and more European the woman looks, the more beautiful she is viewed as being. In essence, beauty standards are deeply rooted in racism and colorism.

I know I'm not telling you anything you weren't aware of when you woke up this morning. Right? The thing is, how many of you buy into this western European standard? I mean, don't believe the hype, don't subscribe to the stereotype. 'Cuz every time you do, you are helping to perpetuate the myth of white supremacy, and this argues against the genetic annihilation of whites. Strong words, huh? Well, as Malcom X said, "Too black, too strong."

Personal experience has taught me to hold my darker-hued sister in great regard. She has endured a lot. I've heard brothers and sisters talk about a person being too dark, having too big a nose, too-nappy hair, or too-large lips. Every time I hear this, I cringe. It is obvious to me that such utterances are outright condemnations of all African physical traits, particular sub-Saharan Africans traits. Traits that most African-Americans can trace in their ancestry. Come on, how can the physical characteristics of the original people be ugly!

Unfortunately, from the cradle to the grave, we are bombarded with the lie that "white is right." This mind-set originated in Europe and has been barbarously spread across the globe. It started during the age of exploration and did the most damage during the years of slavery, imperialism, and colonialism. These actions led to the physical and mental subjugation of people of color worldwide. This subjugation was not based and is not based on one group's superiority or inferiority, but on one group's quest for self-preservation. It is a defense mechanism used to ensure the perpetuation of genetically recessive traits.

The real trip is that the biggest threat to this world order is the African. This is why Africans are the most oppressed people. Basically, the darker and more physically African, the greater the threat. Just think, if the world's people were to come together in peace and love, then what would we be made of? What would we look like?

You dig?

It seems to me that the young African Americans of today define "blackness" in a very superficial way: by one's clothes, one's musical tastes, and of course, by one's skin color. But this all must go if we as a people are to ever love and respect ourselves. I have seen the sorrow in the face of a beautiful ebony woman who realizes that the reason her butterscotch friend is getting hawked by the men is because she's light. I have seen the anguish in the mixed kid who, try as she might, can never succeed at being black enough to be black or white enough to be white. I have seen the names "tar baby," "liver lips," "nap head," "high yellow nigga," and "blackassed, nappy headed bitch" elicit rivers of tears. Honestly, I have seen enough.

Vanessa May is a twenty-three-year-old African American Lover of Life, and student of law at Howard University.

The temptation to remain dysfunctional arises from the fact that we spent so much time and energy getting this way, it feels like a waste sometimes just to throw it all out.

—Conversation with Sharon Armonte, 1992

Maria E. Barron in Mexico at three years old

No Woman's Land

Maria E. Barron

Me rompieron mi lengua.
Dejando en mi boca una caverna
vacia de los sonidos de mi niñez.

They ripped my tongue out.
Leaving my mouth a cavern
empty of the sounds of my childhood.

I was falling into a chasm—deep and dark and cold. I could almost touch the sides, but not quite. I was dropping too fast.

Fear gripped my belly as I walked up to the microphone.

"Voy a probechar (oh my God, I knew that wasn't the right word!) a decir la información en Ingles y en Español."

It was the second day of the Pleasanton Prison multicultural weekend. Workshops were taking place all over the prison, but the women were still sitting in the "Barn," where the main events were presented.

Francoise, our stage manager, rushed up to me, "Maria, they don't understand what's going on. I'll turn the mike on and you tell them, ok?"

All weekend I had counted on my friends Olivia, Juanita, and Linda to do the translating. The prison had close to 40 percent Latinas, and the organizers were committed to translating as much as possible. But I had spoken Spanish only a little here and there, one on one, where I could apologize for my lack of vocabulary.

Language is a giant wound to me. Tears come to my eyes even as I write these words. There is so much anger and pain over the loss of my language and the rape of my soul. There are no words large enough to describe it.

I came to this country at the age of five already beginning to write my name and simple ideas in Spanish. Language mirrors the soul, and my life was filled with music, colors, and passion.

Once here, my stepfather did not allow my mother and me to speak Spanish to one another. This was not done out of meanness. He had the misguided idea that this would facilitate our learning English. Since we lived in Wonderbreadland we would have learned English anyway. Nobody else spoke Spanish.

In second grade, while the other children took naps, I was sent to speech class to rid me of my accent.

("Now, Henrietta, look at me and watch the position of my mouth. Tongue clicking against your upper front teeth—the word is church not shursh.")

I hated placing my mouth in those uncomfortable positions. I hated having to think before I spoke.

Soon, however, those positions became comfortable and my mother tongue receded to a vague memory. The music, colors, and passion also receded. Children don't like to be outsiders. I became assimilated.

Seven years ago I went into recovery. Recovery of my cultural and racial roots was the foundation stone for the recovery of myself.

I went in search of my Latina sisters.

(Pues, Maria, tu eres Chicana o eres Mexicana?")

Chasm time again. I wasn't raised in the Chicana culture, but nor was I raised in Mexico. As I tried to explain, their eyes would glaze over and shift to another, more defined Latina.

The hurt went deep.

I wanted to say, "It wasn't my fault!" I wanted to say, "Please, let me in."

Women would come up to me speaking fluent Spanish, and I would listen intently, willing my mind and heart to remember. Sometimes I was forced to say, "I'm sorry, I don't understand you."

Again, the glazed eyes.

The isolation, the aloneness was so complete. I was in no woman's land, not being white nor being wholly Mexican.

But, I refused to give up. I kept going to Latina functions. I began to be able to say, "I am Mexican-born, United States–raised. I would like to speak Spanish if you don't mind speaking slowly."

Eventually, I found women responding. Not all of them, but I got past the point of needing the approval of the whole Latina community to validate my Mexicaness.

However, when faced with a new community—as I was at the prison—the old fears, the insecurities still come up. Even when they say, "No, no, tu hablas bastante bien," my internal voice says, "Who're you kidding?" It takes only one woman giving that Latina attitude to throw me in that chasm. (Did I say I was over it?)

But I hold on—I keep truckin'. Defining and appreciating Self is difficult when you are bicultural and biclass.

The other day one of my Puerto Rican friends said, "Hey, Maria, you don't speak five-year-old Spanish anymore. You're up to eight years old now."

And I laughed. Humor is essential in the work of reclaiming. Without it, we could drown in our tears. And besides, laughter is a large part of the passion I had lost.

Maria Enriqueta Barron de Gonzales
(gracias a Mercedes Troncosa for her help with the Spanish)

Maria E. Barron is a Mexican-born, United States–raised, bicultural, biclass lesbian woman whose life work is discovering the diversity within herself and her world.

Afterword

Elizabeth Martínez

In late June, 1994 some five hundred civil rights movement veterans including this writer came together in Jackson for the 30th anniversary of the historic Mississippi Summer Project. The 1964 Mississippi project had brought to the state one thousand volunteers, mostly white northerners of college age, to work with mostly local Black activists. With them came an entire nation's horrified attention as jailings, beatings, bombings and murder met efforts to register Black voters or set up Freedom Schools and community centers. The silence protecting southern racist oppression of African Americans finally began to crack; a Voting Rights Act soon became law along with the end of Jim Crow segregation.

At the reunion, a large number of college students attended, most of them from local Black schools. Their anger and energy galvanized us all. At one huge workshop, Black youth took the floor for over an hour while their elders listened to them talk about various experiences of contemporary racism and strategies for change.

Then a young woman among them began to tell how her mother, a Pakistani immigrant, had been fired from her job "because you smell." But the smell, explained the daughter, "came from spices my mother used in traditional Pakistani cooking." You could hear students murmur angrily. "And people told my mother to try harder to learn English, get rid of her accent. But why don't *they* try harder to understand us?" Black students and others burst out clapping loud and long for her anger; they too had known cultural contempt.

My hopes rose in that moment that some youth today might do a better job of crossing the lines between different people of color than most of the previous generation had done. That they might refuse to embrace the hatred for immigrants of color being fostered among U.S. citizens of color by forces that despise and exploit both. That they might grasp the linkage between racial oppression and nationality oppression.

Our times call with new urgency for understanding such issues, for constructing a 21st century solidarity against White Supremacy, a solidarity that has room for growing social complexity. People of color need to turn today's swiftly changing demographics into a source of strength rather than a new round of divide-and-conquer games. "Beware the Oppression

Olympics," as a student I met once said. In the face of escalating racism all over the world, can any of us afford to be made an instrument that sustains White Supremacy through our own ignorance?

No: Asians, Pacific Islanders, and Latinos coming to this country, as my father did, need to learn about the unspeakable racism experienced by African-Americans for centuries—and stand with them against that common enemy. No: African-Americans need to understand the exploitation, abuse and sometimes murder of Latino-Americans and Asian-Americans for not being "real Americans"—not to mention for their lack of European features. None of us escapes the fact that "whiteness" has defined the national identity of the United States since its infancy in a cradle of genocide against the indigenous inhabitants.

(It is my personal dream for everyone of good will to see what's wrong with this country calling itself "America." That name stands for an entire continent: not a single, self-defined nation but a continent, and one overwhelmingly inhabited by people of color. I recognize that longtime usage has locked "America" in place as meaning the U.S.A. I also recognize that indigenous people dislike "America" as a name for the continent, given its European-invader origin. Nevertheless, to protest U.S. usurpation of the term does shine a light in the darkness of Yankee-imposed ignorance.)

How can we help build that 21st century solidarity among people of color? This book points to one of two crucial ways, the way called *listening to others and opening our minds*. We need to hear from all kinds of color, national, and cultural perspectives, or we shall forever subvert our potential for unity. We must look and listen beyond the bipolar model that sees racism only in terms of black-and-white. Elena Featherston's collection of writings by women of color performs this service. She also extends the tradition of such anthologies with her thematic focus on racism and colorism. If we recall such work as that pioneering volume *This Bridge Called My Back*, edited by Gloria Anzaldúa and Cherríe Moraga, we see that a much needed road is being built in recent years, with more and more byways to pursue, and new revelations each time.

We need to listen to so many voices, not only those already known and respected but also the new and less known. Newer voices are the heart of this book and one of its most important gifts, especially in these changing times. The strong presence here of mixed-heritage writers, for example, points to what will be a growing population with its own complex messages.

The other crucial way to build that 21st century solidarity is *fighting together in concrete, daily-life struggles against a common enemy*. For this no substitute exists: we must work out any conflict of differences non-abstractly, face to face. But the two ways should go hand in hand. Then we can learn from having different perspectives, not shy away in fear, contempt, or provincialism. How shall we ever overcome racism and colorism except with human collectivity? How else to know liberation?

Author, teacher of Ethnic and Women Studies, and currently an activist in the San Francisco Bay Area, **Elizabeth Martínez** *worked in the Black civil rights movement with the Student Nonviolent Coordinating Committee (SNCC) and the Chicano movement for years. Her books include* Letters from Mississippi *and* The Youngest Revolution: A Personal Report on Cuba *(under ther name Sutherland), and most recently the bilingual volume* 500 Years of Chicano History in Pictures.

Reading List

This list just scratches the surface—a comprhehensive catalog would be another book—but it can get you started. You can purchase or order these books from Old Wives' Tales, 1009 Valencia Street, San Francisco, CA 94110, (415) 821-4675.

Adelman, Jean, Gloria Enquídanos (Eds.), *Racism in the Lives of Women: Testimony, Theory and Guides to Anti-Racist Practice,* Haworth Press Inc. (forthcoming November, 1994).

Agosin, Marjorie, *Brujas y Algo Mas,* Latin American Literary Review Press, Pittsburgh, PA.

Agosin, Marjorie, *Women of Smoke,* Red Sea Press, Lawrenceville, NJ.

Aguilar-San Juan, Karen, *The State of Asian American Activism & Resistance in the 1990s,* South End Press, Boston, MA.

Alegria, Claribe, *Luisa in Reality Land,* Curbstone Press, Willimantic, CT.

Allen, Paula Gunn (Ed.), *Spider Woman's Granddaughters, Traditional Tales and Contemporary Writing by Native American Women,* Fawcett Columbine, New York, NY.

Allende, Isabel, *Eva Luna,* Bantam Books, New York, NY.

Ansa, Tina McElroy, *Baby of the Family,* Harcourt Brace Jovanovich, San Diego, CA.

Ansa, Tina McElroy, *Ugly Ways,* Harcourt Brace Jovanovich, New York, NY.

Arnot, Madeline, *Race and Gender,* Pergamon Press, Elmsford, NY.

Astorga-Garcia, *Filipina I : Poetry, Drama and Fiction,* Cellar Book Shop, Detroit, MI.

Astorga-Garcia, *Filipina II: An Anthology of Contemporary Women Writers*, Cellar Book Shop, Detroit, MI.

Astrov, Margot, *Winged Serpent: American Indian Prose*, Beacon Press, Boston, MA.

Bambara, Toni Cade (Ed.), *Salteaters*, Random House, New York, NY.

Bataille, Gretchen M., and Charles L. P. Silet, (Eds.), *The Pretend Indians: Images of Native Americans in the Movies*, The Iowa State University Press, Ames, IA.

Bell, Derrick, *Faces of at the Bottom of the Well*, Harper & Row, New York, NY.

Boyd, Julia, *In the Company of My Sisters*, Dutton Books, New York, NY.

Brant, Beth, *A Gathering of Spirit: A Collection by North American Indian Women*, Firebrand Books, Ithaca, NY.

Brown, Elaine, *Taste of Power*, Doubleday, New York, NY.

Brown, Linda, *Rainbow Roun Mah Shoulder*, Ballantine Books, New York, NY.

Busby, Margaret, *Daughters of Africa*, Random House, New York, NY.

Butler, Octavia, *Kindred*, Beacon Press, Boston, MA.

Butler, Octavia, *Parable of the Sower*, Four Walls Eight Windows, New York, NY.

Cameron, Anne, *Daughters of Copper Woman*, Press Gang Publishers, Vancouver, British Columbia, Canada.

Cartier, Xam, *Be Bop Re Bop*, Ballantine Books, New York, NY.

Chin, Chan, Inada, *Aiiieeeee: Anthology of Asian American Writing*, New American Library, New York, NY.

Chin, Chan, Inada, *Big Aiiieeeee*, Penguin Books, New York, NY.

Chirimuuta, R. J. & R. C., *Aids, Africa, and Racism*, Free Assoc. Books, London. (Distributed in the United States by Columbia University Press, NY.)

Christian, Barbara, *Black Feminist Criticism*, Pergamon Press, Elmsford, NY.

Chrystos, *Dream On*, Press Gang Publishers, Vancouver, Canada.

Chrystos, *Not Vanish*, Press Gang Publishers, Vancouver, Canada.

Churchill, Ward, *Indian Are Us? Culture, Genocide in Native North America*, Common Courage Press, Monroc, ME.

Cisneros, Sandra, *My Wicked Ways*, Random House, New York, NY.

Clarke, Cheryl, *Narratives*, Kitchen Table Press, Latham, NY.

Cleage, Pearl, *Deals with the Devil: And Other Reasons to Riot*, Ballantine Books, New York, NY.

Cole, Johnnetta, *Conversations Straight Talk with America's Sister President*, Doubleday, New York, NY.

Collins, Patricia, *Black Feminist Thought*, Routledge, Chapman & Hall, New York, NY.

Coltelli, Laura, *Winged Words: American Indian Writers Speak*, University of Nebraska Press, Lincoln, NE.

Cooper, J. California, *Piece of Mind*, Doubleday, New York, NY.

Cooper, J. California, *Some Soul to Keep*, Saint Martin's Press, New York, NY.

Corpi, Lucha, *Eulogy for a Brown Angel*, Arte Publico Press, Houston, TX.

Cowan, William (Ed.) *Papers of the Twenty-First Algonuian Conference*, Carleton University, Ottawa, Canada.

Cyr, Helen W., *The Third World in Film and Video, 1984–90*, Scarecrow Press, Metuchen, NJ.

Dash, Julie, *Daughters of the Dust*, W. W. Norton, New York, NY.

Davis, Angela, *Women, Culture & Politics*, Random House, New York, NY.

Davis, Angela, *Women, Race & Class*, Random House, New York, NY.

Deavere-Smith, Anna, *Fires in the Mirror: Crown Heights and Other Identities*, Anchor Books, New York, NY.

Deloria, Ella Cara, *Waterlily*, University of Nebraska, Lincoln, NE.

Edmunds, Margot, and Ella E. Clark, *Voices of the Wind: Native American Legends*, Facts on File, New York, NY.

Edrich, Louise, *Love Medicine*, Harper & Row, New York, NY.

El Dareer, Asma, *Woman, Why Do You Weep? Circumcision and Its Consequences*, Zed Press, London.

Faludi, Susan, *Backlash: The Undeclared War Against American Women*, Anchor Books, New York, NY.

Foerstel, Lenora, *Women's Voices on the Pacific: The International Pacific Policy Conference*, Maisonneuve Press, University Park, MD.

Frankenberg, Ruth, *White Women, Race Matters: The Social Construction of Whiteness*, University of Minnesota Press, Minneapolis, MN.

Gaymon, Gloria Leaks, *215 Black Women You Should Know*, National Press, Philadelphia, PA.

Giddings, Paula, *When and Where I Enter: The Impact of Black Women on Race and Sex in America*, Bantam Books, USA/Canada.

Golden, Marita (Ed.), *Wild Women Don't Wear No Blues*, Doubleday, New York, NY.

Gomez, Jewelle, *Forty-Three Septembers*, Firebrand Books, Ithaca, NY.

gossett, hattie, *Presenting Sister No Blues*, Firebrand Books, Ithaca, NY.

Gould, Janice, *Beneath My Heart*, Firebrand Books, Ithaca, NY.

Hagedorn, Jessica, *Dogeaters*, Viking/Penguin, New York, NY.

Hardy-Fanta, Cindy, *Latina Politics, Latino Politics,* Temple University Press, Philadelphia, PA.

Harjo, Joy, *In Mad Love and War*, University Press, New England, Hanover, NH.

Harjo, Joy, *Secrets from the Center of the World*, University of Arizona Press, Tucson, AZ.

Hogan, Linda, *Mean Spirit*, Ballantine Books, New York, NY.

Hong, Maria (Ed.), *Growing Up Asian American*, William Morrow & Co., New York, NY.

hooks, bell, *Ain't I a Woman: Black Women and Feminism*, South End Press, Boston, MA.

hooks, bell, *Black Looks*, South End Press, Boston, MA.

hooks, bell, *Feminist Theory: From Margin to Center*, South End Press, Boston, MA.

hooks, bell, *Sisters of the Yam*, South End Press, Boston, MA.

Hull, Gloria, Patricia Bell Scott, Barbara Smith (Eds.), *But Some of Us Were Brave*, The Feminist Press at the City University of New York, New York, NY.

Hunter-Gault, Charlayne, *In My Place*, Random House, New York, NY.

Hurston, Zora Neale, *Spunk: Selected Stories*, Turtle Island Foundation, Netzahaulcoytl Historical Society, San Francisco, CA.

Hurston, Zora Neale, *Their Eyes Were Watching God*, Harper & Row, New York, NY.

Jaimes, Annette M., *State of Native America: Race*, South End Press, Boston, MA.

James, Joyce, *Spirit, Space and Survival*, Routledge, Chapman & Hall, New York, NY.

Jewell, Terri, *The Black Woman's Gumbo Ya-Ya: Quotations by Black Women*, The Crossing Press, Freedom, CA.

Jordon, June, *Living Room*, Thunder Mountain Press, New York, NY.

Jordon, June, *Technical Difficulties*, Random House, New York, NY.

Kikumura, Akemi, *Through Harsh Winters: The Life of a Japanese Immigrant Woman*, Chandler and Sharp Pulishers, Novato, CA.

Kim, Elaine, *Asian American Literature*, Temple University Press, Philadelphia, PA.

Kingston, Maxine Hong, *Woman Warrior*, Vintage Books, New York, NY.

Kitagawa, Daisuke, *Issei and Nisei: The Internment Years*, Seabury Press, New York, NY.

Kogawa, Joy, *Oasan*, David Godine, Boston, MA.

Kunjufu, Jawanza, *Developing Positive Self-Image and Discipline in Black Children*, African American Images, Chicago, IL.

Lad, Vasant, *Ayurveda: The Science of Self-Healing, a Practical Guide*, Lotus Press, Santa Fe, NM.

La Duke, Betty, *Compañeras: Women, Art & Social Change in Latin America*, City Lights Books, San Francisco, CA.

Lerner, Gerda, *Black Women in White America*, Vintage Books, New York, NY.

Lim, Ginny, *Paper Angels & Bitter Cane*, Kalamaku Press/Le'ahi Press, Honolulu, HI.

Lorde, Audre, *Burst of Light*, Firebrand Books, Ithaca, NY.

Lorde, Audre, *I Am You Sister: Black Women Organizing Across Sexuality*, Kitchen Table Press, Latham, NY.

Lorde, Audre, *Sister Outsider*, The Crossing Press, Freedom, CA.

Lorde, Audre, *Uses of the Erotic*, The Crossing Press, Freedom, CA.

Mankiller, Wilma, *Mankiller: A Chief and Her People*, St. Martin's Press, New York, NY.

McMillian, Terry, *Breaking Ice: An Anthology of Contemporary American Black Fiction*, Viking Penguin, New York, NY.

Miller, Jay (Ed.), *Mourning Dove: A Salishan Autobiography*, University of Nebraska, Lincoln, NE.

Mirikitani, Janice, *Shedding Silence*, Celestial Arts Publishing Co., Berkeley, CA.

Mohr, Nicholasa, *Rituals of Survival*, Arte Publico Press, Houston, TX.

Momaday, Natachee Scott (Ed.), *American Indian Authors*, Houghton Mifflin Company, Boston, MA.

Moraga, Cherrie, *Giving Up the Ghost*, West End Press, Albuquerque, NM.

Moraga, Cherrie, *Loving in the War Years*, South End Press, Boston, MA.

Moraga, Cherie and Gloria Anzaldua, (Eds.), *This Bridge Called My Back: Writings by Radical Women of Color*, Persephone, Watertown, MA.

Morrison, Toni, *Beloved*, New American Library, New York, NY.

Morrison, Toni, *Jazz*, NAL/Dutton, New York, NY.

Morrison, Toni, *Race-ing Justice, Engendering Power: Essays on Anita Hill*, Pantheon Books, New York, NY.

Mukherjee, Bharati, *Middleman & Other Stories*, Fawcett, New York, NY.

Mukherjee, Bharati, *Tiger's Daughter*, Fawcett, New York, NY.

Naff, Alixa, *Becoming American: Early Arab Immigrant Experience*, Southern Illinois University Press, Carbondale, IL.

Naylor, Gloria, *Women of Brewster Place*, New American Library, New York, NY.

Njeri, Itabari, *Every Good-bye Ain't Gone*, Random House, New York, NY.

Otis, Alicia, *Spiderwoman's Dream*, Sunstone Press, Santa Fe, NM.

Rosca, Ninotchka, *State of War*, Simon & Schuster, New York, NY.

Rose, Wendy, *Bone Dance: New and Selected Poems 1965–1993*, University of Arizona, Tucson, AZ.

Salat, Cristina, *Living In Secret*, Bantam Skylark, New York, NY.

Saran, Paramatma, *The Asian Indian Experience in the United States*, Schenckman, Cambridge, MA.

Scott, Patricia Bell, *Life Notes: Personal Writings by Contemporary Black Women*.

Shange, Ntozake, *For Colored Girls Who Have Considered Suicide When the Rainbow Isn't Enough*, MacMillian Publishing Company, New York, NY.

Shange, Ntozake, *Sassafrass, Cypress & Indigo*, St. Martin's Press, New York, NY.

Sharp, Saundra, *Black Women for Beginners*, Writers & Readers Publishing, New York, NY.

Sher, Barbara, *Wishcraft: How to Get What You Really Want*, Ballantine Books, New York, NY.

Silko, Leslie, *Almanac of the Dead*, West End Press, Albuquerque, NM.

Silko, Leslie, *Ceremony*, Penguin Books, New York, NY.

Spallone, Patricia, and Deborah L. Steinert (Eds.), *Made to Order: Myth of Reproductive and Genetic Progress*, Pergamon Press, Elmsford, NY

Spittal Ohsweken, W. G. (Ed.), *Iroquois Women: An Anthology*, Iroqrafts, Ontario, Canada

Srivastava, Atima, *Transmission*, Serpent's Tale, London/New York.

Starhawk, *Truth or Dare: Encounters with Power, Authority and Mystery*, Harper & Row, San Francisco, CA.

Takaki, Ronald, *Pau Hana*, University of Hawai'i Press, Honolulu, HI.

Tall Mountain, Mary, *Light on the Tent Wall: A Bridging*, University of California, American Indian Studies Center, Los Angeles, CA.

Tan, Amy, *Joy Luck Club*, Random House, New York, NY.

Teish, Luisah, *Jambalaya: The Natural Woman's Book of Personal Charms and Practical Rituals*, Harper & Row, New York/London/Sydney/Singapore.

Three Rivers, Amoja, *Cultural Etiquette: A Guide for the Well-Intentioned*, Market Wimmin, Indian Valley, VA.

Trask, Haunani-Kay, *From a Native Daughter: Colonialism & Sovereignty in Hawaii*, Common Courage Press, Monroe, ME.

Trujillo, Carla, *Chicana Lesbians*, Third Woman Press, Berkeley, CA.

Tsukiyama, Gail, *Women of the Silk*, St. Martin's Press, New York, NY.

Uchida, Yoshiko, *Desert Exile: The Uprooting of a Japanese American Family*, University of Washington Press, Seattle, WA.

Vanzant, Iyanla, *Tapping the Power Within: A Path to Self-Empowerment for Black Women*, Writers & Readers, New York, NY.

Walker, Alice, *In Search of Our Mother's Gardens*, Harcourt Brace Jovanovich, San Diego, CA.

Walker, Alice, *Living by the Word*, Harcourt Brace Jovanovich, San Diego, CA.

Walker, Alice, *Possessing the Secret of Joy*, Pocket Books, New York, NY.

Walker, Alice, *Temple of My Familiar*, Pocket Books, New York, NY.

Walker, Alice/Parmar, Pratiba, *Warrior Marks*, Harcourt Brace Jovanovich, New York, NY.

Wallace, Michelle, *Black Popular Culture*, Bay Press, Seattle, WA.

Weglyn, Michi, *Years of Infamy: The Untold Story of America's Concentration Camps*, Macmillian Publishing, Toronto, Canada.

Welie, Alan R. (Ed.), *The Lightning Within: An Anthology of Contemporary Indian Fiction*, University of Nebraska Press, Lincoln, NE.

White, Evelyn C., *The Black Women's Health Book: Speaking for Ourselves*, The Seal Press, Seattle, WA.

Williams, Patricia, *Alchemy of Race & Rights*, Harvard University Press, Cambridge, MA.

Wong, Nellie, *Death of Longsteam Lady*, West End Press, Albuquerque, NM.

Wong, Nellie, Merle Woo, and Yamada, *Three Asian American Writers Speak Out on Feminism*, San Francisco Radical Women, San Francisco, CA.

Wong, Diane and Asian Women United (Eds.), *Making Waves: An Anthology of Writings by and about Asian American Women*, Beacon Press, Boston, MA.

Yamada, Mitsui, *Camp Notes*, Kitchen Table Press, Ithaca, NY.

Yamamoto, Hisaye, *Seventeen Syllables & Other Stories*, Kitchen Table Press, Ithaca, NY.

Resources

A SISTER'S PLACE
3712 N. Broadway, #700
Chicago, IL 60613
(312) 275-1319
A Sister's Place offers safe, comfortable, and affordable guest rooms for women in the Andersonville neighborhood of Chicago. Women traveling to Chicago to visit friends, attend a conference, perform in a play, enjoy some culture, work on a novel, or just get some peace and quiet, stay at A Sister's Place; guestrooms for women in a private flat of a Chicago artist.

ACHÉ
3122 Shattuck Avenue
Berkeley, CA 94705
Aché is an organization for lesbians of African descent. Aché's goals include the documentation of black lesbian herstory and culture, furthering development of artistic, political, and economic resources in the communities, and providing a forum where issues or discussed openly and at an international level. Publishes Aché, a quarterly magazine for the benefit of lesbians of African descent and all Black women. Subscription: Sliding scale $15 – $25/per year.

ALASKA NATIVE SISTERHOOD—CAMP #12
Box 556
Hoonah, AK 99829
(907) 945-3630
Formed to fight discrimination against Native Alaskans, the Sisterhood addresses issues like care of the elderly, education for Native Alaskan children, and subsistence fishing rights.

ASIAN IMMIGRANT WOMEN ADVOCATES
310 8th Street, Suite 301
Oakland, CA 94607
(510) 268-0192
AIWA is committed to the empowerment of women through organizing and education. AIWA's programs include English classes, a food production and packaging cooperative, leadership development, employment training and placement, and social activities.

ASIAN TASK FORCE AGAINST DOMESTIC VIOLENCE
P. O. Box 73
Boston, MA 02120
(617) 338-2350
A coalition of individuals and organizations committed to ending violence against Asian women through outreach and education on domestic violence issues in Asian communities; education and training of mainstream service providers, advocacy for bilingual resources and addressing social structures, ideologies, and behaviors that perpetuate violence against Asian women.

ASIAN WOMEN UNITED
P. O. Box 64078
San Francisco, CA 94164
AWU was founded to promote the social, economic, and general welfare of Asian American women. Active members in the organization include Chinese, Filipino, Japanese, Korean, South and Southeast Asian women who are engaged in research, teaching, writing, advocacy, and community service.

AUNT LUTE FOUNDATION
223 Mississippi Street
San Francisco, CA 94107
(415) 826-1300
This organization publishes multicultural women writers and other voices generally excluded from the mainstream press. Aunt Lute also publishes bilingual books.

BAY AREA NETWORK OF LATINAS
P. O. Box 470321
San Francisco, CA 94117
Formed to foster and promote the social, educational, and economic advancement of Latinas. Programs include quarterly forums on current Latina issues, networking events, and a mentorship program for adolescent Latinas.

BIHA: BLACK INDIAN HISPANIC ASIAN WOMEN IN ACTION
122 West Franklin Avenue, #306
Minneapolis, MN 55404
(612) 870-1193
Established to break down the cultural barriers between communities of color and the community at large. BIHA works with private and public agencies to help them provide services that recognize the needs of people of

color. It has a quarterly newsletter, speakers bureau, and ongoing forums and workshops.

BLACK WOMEN ORGANIZED FOR EDUCATIONAL
DEVELOPMENT
518 17th Street, Suite 202
Oakland, CA 94612
(510) 763-9501
Founded to improve and maintain support systems for low-income and socially disadvantaged African American women. The group has a mentoring program for junior high school girls and ongoing support groups which focus on single parenting, male/female relationships, homelessness, career changes, substance abuse, child/parent relationships.

BLACK WOMEN'S FORUM
3870 Crenshaw Boulevard, Suite 210
Los Angeles, CA 90008
(213) 292-3009
BWF has over one thousand members who run the gamut from students to senior citizens, from high-level executives to women receiving public assistance. These women share a common desire to learn more about the issues and problems facing the Black community locally and nationally.

BLACK WOMEN'S RESOURCE CENTER
518 17th Street, Suite 202
Oakland, CA 94612
(510) 763-9501
An information and referral service for African American women and youth. It provides information on local childcare facilities, job listings, career and academic counseling, and referral to agencies that provide temporary shelter, meals, prenatal care, and treatment for victims of drug, alcohol, or sexual abuse.

BROOMSTICK
OPTIONS for Women Over Forty
582 Market Street, Suite 412
San Francisco, CA 94104
(415) 837-0157
A unique reader-participation quarterly by, for, and about women over forty. A national network printing the work, experience, and thoughts of midlife and long-living women. Individual subscriptions in the United States: $15–$30 annually. Canada: $20–$35, Overseas: $25–$40, all in U.S. funds.

CAMBODIAN WOMEN'S HEALTH PROJECT
150 Tremont Street, 3rd Floor
Boston, MA 02111
(617) 727-7222
This project grew out of concern that few Khmer refugee women use the services of rape crisis centers or battered women's shelters. Support and education is provided in their own language and cultural context.

CHICANA SERVICE ACTION CENTER
134 East 1st Street
Los Angeles, CA 90012
(213) 253-5959
This organization helps with clerical training, GED preparation, job placement, and homeless assistance.

THE CIRCLE
1530 East Franklin Avenue
Minneapolis MN 55404
(612) 879-1760
Native American newspaper published monthly. Subscription fee: individual: $14.00 individual, organization: $16.

Co-MADRES
945 G Street, N.W.
Washington, D.C. 20001
(202) 393-0126
Established in 1977 in El Salvador as an organization of the mothers and relatives of the "disappeared," people murdered for political reasons, during the civil war. Co-MADRES in the United States works to educate and inform U.S. citizens of current events in El Salvador and to develop grassroots support to sustain the work of Co-MADRES in El Salvador.

COUNCIL ON INTERRACIAL BOOKS FOR CHILDREN, INC.
1841 Broadway
New York, NY 10023
The council grew out of a belief that *children must be raised in a bias-free environment* if they are to develop a positive self-identity and openness to people of other backgrounds and beliefs. CIBC makes linkages between racism and other forms of bias—sexism, militarism, ageism, ableism, and homophobia. CIBC also offers antiracist and antisexist curriculum guides, lesson plans, and other teaching materials.

COVERTACTION QUARTERLY
1500 Massachusetts Avenue, N.W., #732
Washington, D. C. 20005
(202) 331-9763
A quarterly magazine monitoring the illegal activities of the U.S. intelligence agencies including the CIA, FBI, NSA, and others. Subscriptions are $22 per as of 1994–1995.

CREATIVE LIVING, INC.
P. O. Box 1519
Forestville, CA 95436
(707) 887-1221
Creative Living offers writing and publishing works in quiet, convenient North Bay locations with writing time outdoors. Workshops are practical, playful, and supportive. Creative Living also provides manuscript consultation; finished works are edited for strength and marketability, then returned with a list of potential publishers.

FEATHERSTON & ASSOCIATES
4104 24th Street, #153
San Francisco, CA 94114
(415) 821-0126
Featherston & Associates is a group of cross-cultural trainers specializing in social and cultural equity for educational, corporate, political, and not-for-profit organizations. Individually and in multicultural teams, group members work to end all forms of oppression (particularly those based on class, economics, status, ethnic and cultural background, sexual orientation, age, physical ability and spiritual beliefs) by establishing candid communications designed to help people understand how biases affect their lives so they can alter personal behavior and implement political change within institutions.

GLOBAL EXCHANGE
2017 Mission Street, Suite 303-B
San Francisco, CA 94110
(415) 255-7296
Global Exchange promotes international grassroots activism through partnership projects, speaking tours for Third World Activists, and "Reality Tours" to Cuba, Southern Africa, Haiti, Mexico, and Appalachia. A subscription to the quarterly newsletter is included in the $35 organization membership fee.

HOT WIRE: THE JOURNAL OF WOMEN'S MUSIC & CULTURE
5210 N. Wayne
Chicago, IL 60640
The only publication devoted to the woman-identified women's music & culture scene.

IMMIGRANT WOMEN'S TASK FORCE
995 Market Street, 11th Floor
San Francisco, CA 94103
(415) 821-4552
Made up of over twenty representatives of women's rights organizations, domestic violence programs, legal assistance projects, and other programs advocating for the special needs of immigrant women.

INDIGENOUS WOMEN'S NETWORK
P. O. Box 174
Lake Elmo, MN 55042
(612) 770-3861
The network was begun to improve the visibility of native women and to apply traditional values in a modern society. Publishes the magazine *Indigenous Woman* twice a year. Become a member (includes subscription): Voting membership (Native women), $15.00 or Supporting membership, $25.00 (Organizations or others). Subscription, 2 issues: U.S. $10.00, Foreign $20.00

INSTITUTE FOR THE HEALING OF RACISM
P.O. Box 2533
Flagstaff, AZ 86003
(602) 526-3315
The institute was established to create dialogs between people from different cultural backgrounds that break down barriers to human communications. The purpose of the institute's workshop is to help individuals realize that we are more alike than we are different, making our diversity our strength.

INTERNATIONAL RESOURCE NETWORK OF WOMEN
OF AFRICAN DESCENT
1208 Clearbrook Drive
Atlanta, GA 30311
(404) 880-8617
Promotes the exchange of ideas and information about research, publications,

programs, projects, activities, and issues of concern of women of African descent. The organization has a membership that spans thirty-seven nations.

KITCHEN TABLE: WOMEN OF COLOR PRESS
P. O. Box 908
Latham, NY 12110
(518) 434-2057
Publishes fiction and nonfiction by women of color. The philosophy of the press is to unite all people of color, not to discriminate on the basis of sexual preference, to eradicate racism, and to work toward a just society.

LA PEÑA CULTURAL CENTER
3105 Shattuck Avenue
Berkeley, CA 94705
(510) 849-2572
La Pena is a bilingual, multicultural center open seven nights a week for concerts, films, dances, classes, and grassroots fund-raising events. Since 1975, more than five hundred community groups have used this space of discussion, information, and debate among different people. The center also has a gift shop, La Tienda, and a restaurant, Cafe Carmelina.

LESBIANS OF COLOR PROGRAM
c/o Pacific Center for Human Growth
2712 Telegraph Avenue
Berkeley, CA 94705
(510) 548-8283
This is a program of Pacific Center for Human Growth. It provides support, counseling, information, and referral, and a safe meeting place for lesbians of color.

MANAVI
P. O. Box 614
Bloomfield, NJ 07003
(908) 687-2662
Manavi is a statewide service organization concerned with the issues and problems of South Asian women in the United States. Principal efforts are dedicated to battered, abandoned, racially and/or sexually harassed, impoverished, or victimized South Asian women. Manavi seeks to create a visible ethnic identity for South Asian women in the United States, and supports struggles for self-reliance in South Asia.

MORENA: WOMEN OF COLOR PRESS
P. O. Box 12964
Berkeley, CA 94701
(510) 549-4710
A bimonthly, bilingual newspaper, in English and Spanish, that offers a forum for political views, a showcase for writers and artists of color, and a listing of services for women of color. Morena has a particular focus on dialogue between Christian and Muslim women.

MOSAIC BOOKS
167 Avenue B
New York, NY 10009
(212) 475-8623
This is a pretty eclectic place: the primary goal is to support writers. A retail bookstore that carries contemporary fiction and poetry, there is also a resource gallery, with new visual arts exhibitions every six weeks, and a reading series which runs from September through May. "Inclusion" is the watchword here.

NAJDA: WOMEN CONCERNED ABOUT THE MIDDLE EAST
P. O. Box 7152
Berkeley, CA 94707
(408) 732-5484
Najda's purpose is to inform Americans about all aspects of the Arab world and to provide assistance to Arab families in need. NAJDA conducts workshops, networks with Arab and American women's groups, and provides education on the Palestinian question and violations of human rights in the Middle East. A newsletter is published four times a year.

NATIONAL BLACK PROGRAMMING CONSORTIUM
929 Harrison Avenue, Suite 101
Columbus, OH 43215
(614) 299-5355
Has two publications—Take One and Take 2. Take 2 takes an in-depth look at contemporary issues in the film/video field and their impact on society and the African American community.

NATIONAL BLACK WOMEN'S HEALTH PROJECT
1237 Ralph David Abernathy Boulevard
Atlanta, GA 30310
(404) 758-9590

The NBWHP exists to define, promote, and maintain health and wellness for African American women and girls. Its overall goal is to empower Black women to take charge of their lives, improve their personal health status, and engage in community-based health promotion activities through self-help and health advocacy. The organization publishes *Vital Signs* three or four times a year.

NATIONAL COALITION BUILDING INSTITUTE
1835 K Street, N.W., Suite 715
Washington, D. C. 20006
(202) 785-9400
(202) 785-3385 - FAX
NCBI is dedicated to ending mistreatment of every group that stems from nationality, race, class, gender, religion, sexual orientation, age, physical ability, job or life circumstance. All programs of NCBI aim to develop a new kind of leader: one who initiates diversity programs, takes principled and courageous stands, can enter the heat of emotional group conflict and build bridges, and models being a fierce ally for all groups.

NATIONAL COUNCIL OF NEGRO WOMEN
101 G Street, NW, Suite 800
Washington, D.C. 20001
(202) 628-0015
NCNW is a council of national organizations and community-based sections that focus on strengthening the Black family, education, and work with women in African countries. NCNW's International Division participates in projects responding to the needs of women in Senegal, Egypt, Botswana, Mozambique, and Angola. NCNW publishes a quarterly magazine, *Sisters*.

NATIVE AMERICAN WOMEN'S HEALTH EDUCATION RESOURCE CENTER
P. O. Box 572
Lake Andes, SD 57356
(605) 487-7072
This resource center provides education about health, nutrition, and reproductive rights to Native American women in South Dakota. The center also has a child development program and a battered women's shelter.

PACIFIC CENTER FOR HUMAN GROWTH
2712 Telegraph Avenue
Berkeley, CA 94705
(510) 548-8283
PCHG offers counseling, informal peer group sessions, information, referrals, HIV advocacy, 12-step recovery programs, and other support services by and for sexual minorities. The center has more than twenty-five programs which include: Alanon, HIV/AIDS support, incest survivor support, transvestite/transexual support, sex and love addiction counseling, bisexual support, gays and lesbians of color support, and gay youth rap groups. PCHG also has a speakers bureau and training programs.

REVOLUTIONARY SISTERS OF COLOR
P.O. Box 2298
Jamaica Plain, MA 02130
(202) 872-1770
A socialist feminist organization with an international, multi-issue, activist agenda. RSC works toward our physical survival; the full political, economic, and social power of our people; the independence of "Third World" countries, and by extension, the affirmation and respect for our cultures and histories; and the democratic community control of production, wealth, and natural resources.

SAGE WOMEN'S EDUCATIONAL PRESS, INC.
P. O. Box 42741
Atlanta, GA 30311
(404) 681-3643
Sage is a biannual scholarly journal about Black women. It is housed at the Women's Research & Resource Center, Spelman College, and its articles are geared to students, teachers, researcher, policy makers, and anyone interested in Black women's lives.

SAKHI FOR SOUTH ASIAN WOMEN
P. O. Box 1428, Cathedral Station
New York, NY 10025
(212) 695-5447
Sakhi is a collective whose main goals are to raise issues of concern of women of Pakistani, Indian, Bangladeshi, Sri Lankan, and Nepalese origin. The primary focus of the group is to work with battered women and engage in community education around domestic violence. Sakhi provides counseling, legal advocacy, and shelter referral.

SPEAK OUT!
2215-R Market St., #520
San Francisco, CA 94114
(415) 864-4561
A political speakers bureau providing professional speakers (historians, journalist, economists, etc.) and artist (poets, writers, musicians, etc.) for campus, community, and labor audiences throughout the United States and Canada. They can help you organize for an individual speaker or for a lecture series.

WAI'ANAE WOMEN'S SUPPORT GROUP
84-766 Lahaina Street
Wai'anae, HI 96792
(808) 696-4913
This group was formed to promote the self-sufficiency of Native Hawaiian women and their families, harmonious community living, support for world peace and women worldwide. They have published women's stories and poetry in *A Time for Sharing* and conducted poetry workshops.

WOMAN OF POWER MAGAZINE
P.O. Box 2785
Orleans, MA 02653
(508) 240-7877
Each issues celebrates international visions of feminism, spirituality, and politics that are transformational, creative, growth-centered, and empowering.

WOMANSPEAK
2462 Matlija Canyon
Ojai, CA 93023
(805) 646-9721
A rites-of-passage organization devoted to empowering women of all ages through spending time in the wilderness, both in a supportive community and alone.

WOMEN AGAINST RACISM
130 N. Madison
Iowa City, IA 52242
(319) 335-1486
A group of multiracial women working in concert to dismantle racism and other oppressive behaviors, personally and institutionally.

WOMEN AND AIDS RESOURCE NETWORK
30 3rd Avenue
Brooklyn, NY 11211
(718) 596-6007
WARN provides HIV/AIDS counseling and education.

WOMEN OF COLOR CENTER
University of California, Berkeley
312 Eshleman Hall
Berkeley, CA 94720
(510) 643-9921
This is a student-initiated service group that sponsors an annual women-of-color retreat and an internship program that links women of color students with community organizations.

WOMEN OF COLOR RESOURCE CENTER
2288 Fulton Street, Suite 103
Berkeley, CA 94708
(510) 848-9272
WCRC makes comprehensive, up-to-date information and analysis accessible to social-change activists engaged in organizing to improve the condition of women of color. They publish the *Director of Women of Color Organizations and Projects.*

photo by Lorene Warwick

Elena Featherston works as a writer, lecturer, workshop leader and the producer/director of the award-winning documentary Alice Walker: Visions of the Spirit. *Ms. Featherston is the founder of FEATHERSTON AND ASSOCIATES, a group of cross-cultural trainers specializing in gender and racial equity for educational, corporate, political and not-for-profit organizations.*

Since 1982 she has lectured on social theory at campuses throughout the United States and Europe. She is a counselor and group leader for a variety of cross-cultural concerns: sexism, racism, women's spirituality, gay oppression, Black women's history, multiculturalism, childrearing, sexuality, and art as a tool of resistance.

A long-time activist, Ms. Featherston is involved in many political movements including Civil and Human Rights, the Women's Movement, the Anti-Nuclear Movement and movements for Freedom, Peace and Justice in South Africa. Most recently she has taught racial equity seminars to Green Party members throughout Germany.

Her current film and video project is The Politics of Intimacy: Interracial Relationships, *an exploration of relationships between women of color and white men.*